TESTIMONIALS

Remarkable Leadership Lessons is like *Chicken Soup for the Soul*, but for businesses.

Cazzell Smith
Media Professional

As a former NC State Senator, a husband, father, a businessman, and a neighbor, every day I am challenged to open my mind to the possibility that there is another side here... another point of view that has to be included in my decisions. This book gives hope to all, that each conversation can change a mind, open a heart, and change your situation.

Joel Ford
Former NC State Senator, SVP Sales and Operations

So glad Denise decided to finally write this book. But a book can only give you a sense of what women need to learn to lead well. If you get to work with her, you'll learn how to find your passion, develop your innate ability to lead, and with gentle guidance make progress on your career goals. This book gives hope that anyone can find their passion no matter what your work situation is.

Julia Paul
Director, Community Outreach

I worked with Denise for about a year. At first, I was unsure about working with her. After all, I had been the CFO for a number of years. But our time together proved invaluable. Women, in particular, need to have someone who can help them cut through the beliefs and habits that stifle growth. Read the stories. See yourself in them, and grow.

Heather Franklin
EVP, Finance

Adapt, change, or die—that is the adage. Everything has changed, so why should we stay the same? Denise's book will show everyone stuck in a rut that change isn't something to be feared but embraced. We learn and grow by stepping out of our comfort zone. This book will give you the push to take that leap of faith.

Jeffrey Hayzlett
Primetime TV & Podcast Host, Speaker, Author,
and Part-Time Cowboy

I found *Remarkable Leadership Lessons* to be lively, clear, entertaining, and easy to read. It is food for thought about the way people focus, plan, organize, network, receive guidance and fulfill their aspirations particularly in corporate America, but with broader implications as well. Your personal experiences of receiving the brunt of racial ignorance and discriminatory attitudes were particularly eye-opening. Thank you for showing me something within myself that is a point of agony, that I can now bring to the forefront and heal.

William Spencer
Security Professional

REMARKABLE
LEADERSHIP
LESSONS

REMARKABLE
LEADERSHIP
LESSONS

Change Results
One Conversation at a Time

DENISE J. COOPER

PYP

PUBLISH
YOUR
PURPOSE
PRESS

Publish Your Purpose Press
141 Weston Street, #155
Hartford, CT, 06141

PUBLISH
YOUR
PURPOSE
PRESS

The opinions expressed by the Author are not necessarily those held by Publish Your Purpose Press.

Ordering Information: Quantity sales and special discounts are available on quantity purchases by corporations, associations, and others. For details, contact the publisher at orders@publishyourpurposepress.com.

Edited by: August Li
Cover design by: Brilliant Creative Studio
Typeset by: Medlar Publishing Solutions Pvt Ltd., India

Printed in the United States of America.
ISBN: 978-1-951591-46-5 (paperback)
ISBN: 978-1-951591-47-2 (ebook)

Library of Congress Control Number: 2020916931

First edition, December 2020

The mission of Publish Your Purpose Press is to discover and publish authors who are striving to make a difference in the world. We give marginalized voices power and a stage to share their stories, speak their truth, and impact their communities. Do you have a book idea you would like us to consider publishing? Please visit PublishYourPurposePress.com for more information.

DEDICATION

The anecdotes in this book are but a small slice of my experiences interspersed with accounts of people I've known past and present. I honor those who came before me and those who will read our stories and in them, find hope for our future.

TABLE OF CONTENTS

SECTION II
MINDSET, BACKGROUND, CULTURE GOING FROM ME TO WE

SECTION III
INFLUENCING AND CHANGING OTHERS

SECTION IV
LEADERSHIP TRAINING AND ORGANIZATIONAL DEVELOPMENT

FOREWORD

It was a surprise and an honor when Denise asked me to write the foreword for this book. I've known Denise Cooper for over 12 years and for several years she was my executive coach.

She was there when I needed an ear to think through the implications of my decisions and she was there helping me navigate the perils of leadership. Executive leadership really is a lonely place. It's lonely because everyone—shareholders, investors, board members and employees—look to the senior executives to be decisive, project an air of confidence, and in some cases, be clairvoyant.

As an African American man, I've learned to gracefully handle subtle and not so subtle forms of racism, insensitivity and benevolence that disempowers.

There were situations when my "uniqueness" was valued and served me well, and other times when it didn't. The many roles and personas I thought I had to take on taught me to be cautious with whom I shared my thoughts, ideas, plans, frustrations and doubts.

From my coaching sessions with Denise, I still apply many of the insights and lessons. For example, solutions to my life's challenges are best resolved by exploring my inner thoughts, beliefs, and desires to understand what's serving my higher purpose and intent or not. Leadership is a singular persona yet requires us to give attention to both mindfulness (being) and demonstration (doing) to positively impact self, others and organizations.

Being in a senior executive leader position, like any form of influencing, requires a great deal of faith in the people around you. You have to cultivate the environment around them so that they will rise to the occasion, tell the truth, do the right thing when you can't see them, and most importantly, have the right mindset (disciplined habits of thinking) that ensures follow-through on the strategic plan.

Today, and as it was then, change is all around. Too many industries are being disrupted by technology, globalism, changing political ideologies and climate change. It is essential for executive leaders to have continual self-care so that they themselves are primed and equipped to empower their organization's wellbeing at any given time or in any type of situation.

This book is filled with stories of how Denise has helped her clients clarify what they really wanted, and how they fortified their ability to express their values and beliefs. These stories can help you name the risks and rewards received when one chooses to lead.

Christopher Powell
CEO, Talmetrix

PREFACE

It's 2:00 a.m. and my aging mom, who lives with me, has had a bad night. I've been exercising her every few hours because her osteoporosis is getting worse, and if she isn't limber, her bones will become too fragile. I'm exhausted but can't sleep, so I am hoping writing inspiration will begin to flow. The laptop is just a white light with a hypnotizing flashing cursor icon screaming *type, type, type*.

Why, as so many people have before me, do I find myself sitting in front of my computer staring at a blank screen, attempting to put my lifetime of experience into a book? Because, every time I speak in front of a group, I get asked for my book. "No book," I say.

"Oh no... You have to have a book," they try to persuade me. "We want to take all that you told us today and put it into action! We love your DENISEisms. PLEASE write a book!"

With the encouragement of a few published authors affirming that my stories will help people, the enthusiasm of coaching clients who believe their stories can teach lessons they wish they'd learned earlier, and bits of wisdom gleaned from the twenty-five years (that's all I'll admit to), of working with and for people, I am embarking on this new experience with admitted trepidation. My "teachers" have been humbly brilliant, great leaders (with and without the title), kind, insightful, and the best mentors anyone could ever have in their life. However, it wasn't until the last eleven years that I gained a deeper understanding of what they were trying to teach me.

Tracy, a branding expert and friend of mine, said "personal change is hard, and frankly, not commonly undertaken. It is however, entirely possible. And to have a good coach to help develop your own insight about what can be improved, how to attack it and make true change, is very helpful."

The stories and ideas that I am presenting for your reading enjoyment stem from my work with people much like you: People struggling to figure out how to find a sense of peace, satisfaction, career success, and ultimately, how to become impactful leaders.

These stories reflect a variety of desires. Some people want to be CEO or in a leadership position where they are responsible for the lives of others. Some want to work for someone who values their contribution, helps them grow professionally, encourages them to feel the joy of playing a meaningful part in something that matters, or have a career that allows them to be financially fit. The challenge is:

"Career Management Has Changed
and You Didn't Get the Memo."

The first lesson you should learn, is that we are all leaders. Every day we influence and are responsible to and for someone. Our decisions impact the lives of so many, and too often leadership is defined by your title or job. Each of us is a leader, and if you believe that, then you know that your job is to get better at influencing others.

Each of us spends a great deal of our day determining what must be done, influencing others to accomplish all or some of what needs to be done, following up, and/or ensuring follow through. If you're a parent, you're leading your children. If you have friends, if you're surrounded by family, then you are trying to influence them to be kind to each other, work together, have fun together, and support each other. If you're one of the estimated 54 million people in

America who provide care for a chronically ill, disabled, or aged family member or friend during any given year, you're taking the lead role, spending an average of twenty hours per week, going on doctor visits, providing meals, doing shopping, handling finances, hygiene, etc. If you work with others at some point during the day, you are influencing them to do something for or with you. Each and every one of us has a multitude of opportunities to make a difference in someone's life.

This book is about how you can lead others, so you achieve better results. You'll read the stories and situations of people who are facing the same challenges you face at work, finding work, or making the decision to leave a job.

There are stories of executives, team leaders, managers, and supervisors who are genuinely interested in being better leaders, designing better workplace cultures, and being socially responsible citizens.

Leading is a choice. It is a contact sport. You have to practice it to get better, and getting better is a lifelong process. Each of us is responsible for navigating the political waters and changing social, technological, and economic landscapes. We are responsible for seeking out, asking for, and developing the skills, knowledge, and abilities that allow us to reinvent ourselves—all so that we can enjoy the freedom to choose where, for whom, and what work matters to us.

Denise J. Cooper

DENISE COOPER:
HOW I CAME TO RECOGNIZE
REMARKABLE

I didn't start out in the world on Easy Street. I grew up in a segregated Chicago neighborhood full of professionals. Black doctors, dentists, business owners of all sorts. Both my parents worked hard to make sure we had what we needed to grow up knowing we were loved. They took every opportunity to teach us how to thrive in a world that first judged you by the way you looked. If you were lucky, the "outside world"—that part of the world where white people lived—was a place you passed through. My siblings and I woke to a nutritious breakfast, went to school, and came home with strict rules about finishing our homework, helping with chores, and spending time with family.

My mother and father didn't have money to send me to college, but it was clear that they expected me to succeed and do something with myself. I became comfortable with not having material possessions and spent my time reading and learning. I dreamed of what I could do, who I would become.

In contemplating my future, it seemed in that time, that I had two options. I was either going to be a secretary, or a teacher. Since I was exceptionally good at secretarial skills, and I didn't have any money to continue my education to become a teacher, the secretarial route seemed the way to go.

One day a guy came to my school and gave a presentation on why we should all go to college. Everybody around me was excitedly picking out places they wanted to go. But there was no way I could go, because my parents couldn't afford it. Along with a few friends in the same boat, I went up to the man afterwards and asked what we should do. He said to us, "If you want to go, pick a school that is not in Illinois and you'll wind up getting scholarships." It planted a seed in our heads, so we started talking about going away to school as a new option.

One day, my friends and I were throwing darts at a map of the USA. If we were going to go somewhere, where should it be? Seemed like throwing darts was as good a method for finding the answer to that big question as any other! I threw a dart and it landed on Sioux Falls, South Dakota, so I applied!

Let me just say that growing up in Chicago, you believed the rest of the world looked pretty much like "this." When you watched TV, everything you saw looked like Chicago, New York, or Los Angeles: big cities, and diverse both racially and culturally. I never even considered that there might not be any people like me outside of the big city!

I had not traveled to many places other than Little Rock, Arkansas (where my father was born), and Parkin, Arkansas (where my mother grew up and her father lived). And although it was the South, the population seemed the same as in my world back in Chicago—I saw black and white people when I was there.

In July, a college called Augustana in South Dakota sent me a letter saying they had a place for me. I was the recipient of a four-year full-ride scholarship! I was elated. Yahoo! I was going to college! I ran into the kitchen to tell my parents, but could not understand why they were not jumping up and down with excitement. Why they looked at each other, then at me, and gave me that fake smile that said they were not totally on board with my new adventure. I was a bit confused but determined to go to college. I had done what they asked of me—I found a way to go to college without them having to pay, and they were not going to stop me. Nor, by the way, did they really try to. Looking back, I can only imagine how torn they were inside knowing that I was heading out into a more rural, possibly racist, potentially unwelcoming community.

In September, my mother and father took me to the Greyhound bus station. There was one other woman, Sheila Brown, waiting to make the journey to South Dakota too. I learned she was a junior at Augustana and she was black. So what did I think? I figured there would be a lot of us there!

It didn't even occur to me to worry about anything other than having the right clothes packed and whether or not I brought the school supplies I needed. As well as, was I going to meet men there? I thought my mother and father were nervous because every parent is nervous sending their kids off to college. And here they were, sticking me on a bus with a suitcase and not much else, to head off to a part of the country no one we knew had ever seen or been to before. In hindsight, my parents must have had an intense level of anxiety as I boarded that bus!

When Sheila and I arrived, even after sitting for twelve hours on a bus, I was buzzing with nerves and excitement. We stepped off the bus, collected our luggage, and found a taxi to take us to the dormitory. Sheila was assigned to be a dorm counselor, so we had to get settled in early.

When other students started arriving, I noticed they were all white. And I'm not talking about Chicago white or New York white. I'm talking about White, white. The kind of white person who is uncomfortably curious and naïve around you because they've never interacted with a black person before.

In all, there were five other black women at the college. Unexpectedly, I found out that all the men were actually a mile down the road. The black guys down the road on the other campus were all jocks. The only reason they came to Sioux Falls College was to play sports. That was it. Most of the black folks around the area were recruited for that reason. Eventually, though, I met a few other black people that came, like me, on a scholarship.

My real-life education started right away. The school had a program where out-of-town students were assigned local adoptive parents. These families would host you for holidays and make sure you got settled in, shown around the town, and were given the low-down on where to go to get everything you needed. They made sure you weren't feeling lonely, being away from family and all.

The intention was for me to live in the dorm, but my adoptive family would have me over for Thanksgiving, Christmas, Easter, and any kind of holiday events. It was assumed that we couldn't afford to go back and forth to our families for holidays, like the students living nearby could.

The school was Lutheran, so church on Wednesdays and Sundays was required, and our adoptive families were to be our hosts for those services and Sunday dinners as well. In those days the Lutheran college expected you to attend services.

The day I showed up to meet my new family (after talking to them several times on the phone, where they seemed to be really polite people), they turned and walked away as soon as they saw me. At the time, as my host "family" walked off into the sunset, it didn't hit me that that was an odd thing. I never saw them again.

Momentarily struck by the rudeness of being abandoned by this new supposed "family," I recognized that the people who were important to me (my family from Chicago), set the context and expectations of my success, not some people I never knew. I had arrived on campus to get an education and that was what I was going to do, with or without an adoptive family!

As a stranger in a strange land, left to my own devices, I called on and applied the guidance and lessons I had learned from family,

Girl Scouts, church, and teachers to help me to achieve my ultimate ambitions.

REMARKABLE LEADERSHIP LESSONS

- Expecting great things from people will lead to people expecting great things from themselves.
- Nothing is more powerful than your expectations. Expectations of yourself and others determine what options and choices you have within reach.
- Once you have set your expectation, nothing and no one will be able to deter you. You know that turning back is not going to get you to the goal, so even if it's uncomfortable or simply unfamiliar, you keep moving forward. You will find a way.

___

DENISEism:
You Don't Know What You Don't Know

___

For the most part, Jasmine and I had caramel, deep-colored skin. So, I literally was one of the darkest people in South Dakota at that time. Jasmine (6'1") and I (5'1") [Laurel & Hardy] decided to stay on campus during the summer.

Summer students would head out onto the campus greens all lathered up in suntan lotion. Embracing the customs of our new surroundings, Jasmine and I decided we were going to do this too. While we were sitting there getting tanned with everyone else, two of our dormmates said, "What are you all doing out here?"

And we told them, "We're out here getting sun."

They said, "You don't need to get any sun!"

And I, employing my Chicago sass, answered, "That's where you're wrong. If we don't get ten days of sun every year, we turn white... like you." We didn't think that she would actually believe that. But she did.

One day my dorm advisor said, "What the hell did you tell these people?"

And I said, "What the hell are you talking about?" She proceeded to tell us there was a rumor that black people can turn white. See the bottom of the feet? That's proof! Another one of those teachable moments! I realized people's reactions were often based on misinformation or twisted information. They learn one nugget that they are trying to process. They have to generalize the information because a person's brain eats up so much of their energy that it cannot process everything in a linear fashion. The brain is wired to process information in a quick way. We make assumptions, decisions, and choices every day, all day based upon our habits.

This lawn-lesson also taught me that I shouldn't assume that white people know ANYTHING about us, at all. Thus, later, when I extrapolated this into the human resources world, I recognized that you can't assume that any person with whom you work (commute, live next door to, etc.) understands or shares your point of view.

Observationally, I could see that was the reason we tended to hire people who were just like us—Not just physically, but also from similar types of neighborhoods, schools, sports involvement, income bracket and so on. I know I was successful being the "only" (the only African-American woman usually) in many organizations because I learned that lesson early on. Somehow, we have to find a story to let people connect to us, so that people will recognize, "You're just like me."

REMARKABLE LEADERSHIP LESSONS

- People's reactions are often based on misinformation or twisted information.
- Like searches for like. People are attracted to what is familiar because it makes them feel safe. Somehow, individuals have to find a shared story to let people recognize, "You're just like me."
- You can't assume that any other person understands or shares your point of view. Having some process for impartial mediation can allay miscommunication and confusion within a workforce.

CODE SWITCHING

When you become the "only," there are a lot of challenges. In an effort to blend in, you can lose your identity. The first time I came home from college after my freshman year and went to talk to my grandmother, I was so excited to tell her about the science program I was going through that I didn't realize I had started talking, "white." She said, "Baby, you're not with them white folks. You can talk like us."

The ability to talk "like us" at home and then "like us" in the work environment is Code Switching. Code Switching is something I had to learn to deal with in order to be able to connect. People who are challenged with Code Switching often have difficulty getting along with the group.

I remember exactly when I made the decision that I wasn't going back to my neighborhood in Chicago after I graduated. My experiences at school, and then within the jobs I held, took me to a whole different place. I really liked being who I was becoming. I liked traveling around America. I liked talking to all different kinds of people. I set an intention of seeing all fifty states before I died. I wanted to see and experience as much as I could. And I knew, regrettably, that my family and the people in my home neighborhood would not necessarily understand the desire to travel and be around people who were different from us.

When I left school, I noted that several African American men (guys who also came on scholarship) chose to stay in South Dakota, marry white women, create families and build community. In Midwestern America where I grew up, my abilities were prejudged by my skin color before they got to know me, but there, in the West, we were not shackled by, or defined by our skin color, or by some perception of a previous experience. People had to take us as we are, because they had no reference points to take us any other way. As I traveled to the surrounding states, I realized that I wasn't defined solely by how I looked. Stereotypes were different and could easily be corrected when wrong or supported when right.

If people didn't like me in these western towns, it was no different than if they didn't like another white person. I was a human first, African American second. Or I was just somebody from a city. Or another demographic like religion or income or profession. But a person would have to talk to me before they knew that information, before they could put me into the relatable or unrelatable box. People came to me with a blank slate, open to hearing about me before judging me. In this situation one could use it or abuse it. In some cases, I used it, and in some cases, I abused it, to be perfectly honest.

It's important to understand that a good coach is able to translate all of the Code Switching and diverse backgrounds and challenges, and help you and your team understand when other people are doing it. For the majority of dysfunctional work environments, that's what is needed. The biggest part of the problem that I see is figuring out where and how to ask questions that feel really insensitive. Because once you have the answers or develop a rapport, you can create a more honest relationship. When one carries around assumptions, there may be misunderstandings. You can choose better outcomes.

EXAMPLES OF QUESTIONS
WE FEEL UNCOMFORTABLE ASKING:

From a White Person to a Black Person

- What does your hair feel like?
- Why do Black people sit at the same table for lunch?
- How do we get more Black people to apply for our jobs?
- Why do Black women seem so angry when they talk?
- What sport did you play?
- What should I call you, Black, African American, Person of Color, Colored, Negro, or something else?
- Why is it okay for Black people to use the word N*gger in songs but it's a problem if a White person does it?
- Why are black people still angry and mad? So much has been achieved. It's not perfect but it's progress.
- Have you experienced racism?
- Why do we need to take down confederate monuments?
- If I make a mistake will you tell me?
- Are Black people more sexual or better at sex?

Questions Black People Have for White People

- Why is a big butt or hips attractive on a White woman but not on a Black woman?
- Why do White people call it discovering something when they steal it from another culture?
- Why is White crime considered an isolated incident and Black crime is about everyone Black?
- Why do you consider the statistics about racist acts, violence against Black people, and health disparities not credible?

Asian Questions for White People

- Why do you think every Asian person is Chinese?
- Why is a film only diverse if it has black people in it?
- Why do you think if you eat Chinese food you know a lot about us?

- Why do you think every Asian person is an immigrant even when I tell you I was born in Chicago or New York?
- Why are you surprised that I can speak English so well?
- Why do you think all Asians are tech or math geniuses?

Latino Questions for White People

- Why are we all lumped together in one category called Latino?
- Why do you assume that just because I'm dark-skinned, I'm black?
- Why is your first assumption that I am undocumented?

Straight Questions Directed to LGBTQA+

- Is there such a thing as "gaydar?"
- How do you know you really are LGBTQA+?
- Why do you feel you need Pride month?
- Why do you have to flaunt your sexuality?
- What do your parents think of your choices?
- Would you decorate my home/office for me?
- Do you have any makeup/style/decorating/cooking tips?
- Don't you think you're too young or just confused? Isn't it a phase you're going through?

LGBTQA+ to Straight/Cisgender People

- Why do straight people assume if I have sex with the opposite sex I'll be cured?

The educational moments I had during my years in South Dakota, outside the book learning, were all about communication and being able to learn about others. Those experiences help me coach my clients in how to use communication techniques to build relationships, mend fences, and create harmony on a team. Allowing people to ask their questions, giving them space to learn that different is not bad, and creating a safe space for uniqueness, helps to foster teamwork, cooperation, and mutual support.

REMARKABLE LEADERSHIP LESSONS

- If people are encouraged to physically talk to others (instead of keeping their heads in computers and devices all the time), they will know if someone is relatable or unrelatable. If people are unable to communicate, they make assumptions based on what they see on the outside (clothing, jewelry, appearance, grooming, mannerisms) which could lead to conflict.
- Different is not bad. Create a safe space for uniqueness, foster teamwork and cooperation, encourage/reward mutual support.
- Use communication to encourage coworkers to learn about each other. Perhaps a newsletter with fun facts about people in each department, a puzzle with answers designed to help give insights to people's lives outside work (find commonality), recognition for achievements in and out of the business environment, rewards for excellent support of coworkers in need, etc.

SOPHOMORE YEAR
IN SOUTH DAKOTA

DENISEism:
We are all blank slates waiting for life to
write the story. What story has life taught you?

In my sophomore year at university in South Dakota, I decided to join the girls' volleyball team. Becky Walnut, the coach, was from North Dakota. She grew up and lived on a ranch and was very athletic. Sports-were-her-life, salt of the earth kind of woman. She took me under her wing and taught me how to play collegiate volleyball.

I played center and right guard because, though tiny in stature, I could jump pretty high. We were scrimmaging before a big game one day and I went for a ball, my knee pads slid off, and I banged up my knee pretty badly. The skin came off and it was bleeding. It really wasn't that big a deal to me. It was like any child falling down and skinning a knee.

Across the line I could hear Becky saying, "Are you okay?"

And I said "Yeah, I'm fine," as I got back to my feet, adjusted my shorts, and was ready to play.

Becky came over because she could see that my knee was bleeding, and she wanted to make sure I really was fine. She told me to sit down so she could examine the wound.

When she looked more closely at my knee, she gasped, "Oh my God, you're white under there!"

I just stared up at her. When the players heard what the coach said, every other girl on the team ran over to see that I was, indeed, white under the skin! The tissue was white! It was at that moment that the whole team realized the color of my skin was on the surface, and underneath, I was exactly like them!

I am still amazed that people in school with me in South Dakota literally didn't know what to think. There was an absence of historical reference for them to grab on to because they had no former interactions with anyone who looked like me before meeting me.

I heard comments like, "Oh my God, you bleed red!" and "Oh my God, you're just like us!" I had been playing with these women for the whole year! "She's just like us" really stayed with me.

After this incident, I changed, because I had gained an awareness that there was (and is) no place where white people can ask any kind of questions to learn about these things. None. No matter where you are. With political correctness, there are some things that you naturally want to know, but you can't ask because it's a political hot button. Unlike children, who can just blurt out questions for adults to answer, adults don't have a safe place to do the same.

REMARKABLE LEADERSHIP LESSONS

- We, as humans, no matter how or where we were raised, are more alike than different from each other.
- People only know and internalize what they've learned, and if businesses want to embrace their employees and create a harmonious workplace, there should be space made for people to learn

about their coworkers. Celebrating commonalities and shared experiences can reduce the learned negative stereotypes.

- In the best places to work, executives are able to ask questions about what they don't know, when not knowing the answers can be uncomfortable. Leaders need to admit when they don't know the answer and feel safe doing that. Stepping into the unknown, publicly, teaches others that it is safe to be curious, vulnerable, and an imperfect human being.

"PEOPLE LIKE YOU"

When I started college, I thought I would end up as a chemistry major. But the chairman of the department, my professor, kept giving me flunking grades. I couldn't understand why as I was studying like everyone else; I was doing well in my other classes. I finally went to him and asked, "What's going on?"

He just looked at me and said, "You people will never be a chemist. You people just don't have it in you."

I don't know if he said it out of malice; I don't know if he did it from ignorance. I was getting the correct answers on my tests, but when I wrote and submitted my papers, he said they weren't good enough. I knew I was never going to graduate with a degree in chemistry as long as he was the chairman of the department. I still don't know if it was because I was a woman, because I was black, because I wasn't from South Dakota, because I was a heathen since I didn't go to a Lutheran (or any) church, or because I didn't grow up with money and was at school on a scholarship?

The whole experience reminded me of what I experienced in Chicago. There were individuals in Chicago who would say to people from my community and my family, when they were seeking employment or a business loan, or to rent an apartment,

"We don't care. No matter what, you don't qualify." I had a similar experience when I was in Arkansas. "Keep your mouth shut" was the message.

The ghost of Emmett Till, a fifteen-year-old African American boy who was beaten and mutilated in Mississippi in 1955 because he spoke to a white woman, still lived very deep within me. There are some places you just don't have a business going to.

So, I switched from chemistry and declared that I would be an elementary and special ed teacher. Ms. Louise (aka Mom) always taught me, "You get lemons, you make lemonade." Her message to me: "Don't bring your butt home without a degree."

REMARKABLE LEADERSHIP LESSONS

- When you run into an unmovable roadblock, don't waste your time and energy trying to remove the blockage. Create a work-around to get you to your end goal.
- Everyone judges and is judged and stereotyped. It's part of human conditioning. The challenge facing all of us is that we are responsible for changing our minds when it is warranted. When we change our minds, we change our behaviors. We humans cling to old truths; change takes time. Each of us needs to ask, "What does it take for me to change my mind?"

JUNIOR YEAR IN SOUTH DAKOTA

"Kids say the darnedest things."

Art Linkletter

Before you do student teaching to get your degree in Education, you have to do student observation time in several schools. I showed up on my first day at a kindergarten class in a public school. There was one little boy who wouldn't come near me. The other kids were fine, but this one boy wasn't having anything to do with me. Even over time, there was nothing it seemed I could do to have this boy interact with me. I was there twice a week, and when I'd get close, he'd run away.

I finally talked to the classroom teacher and asked her, "So what's the deal?"

She said, "I don't know. He's not telling me anything. Nothing. Zip." One day I was reading a book to the kids after we had finished the math lesson, and this distant boy looked at me and blurted out, "Do you EVER take a bath?" Oh my! Gotta love kindergarten.

I answered, "Yes."

"You're a liar," he said.

"Why would you say that?" I asked, really curious.

"Because you look like dookie!" he exclaimed, comparing me to poop.

"I look like dookie?" I puzzled back.

Over on the side of the room, the teacher started freaking out. "Don't say that!" she shouted as she came closer. "That's very rude," she lectured the boy, leaning down toward him.

But, to me, the kid's only five years old. I looked at him and I said, "Would you like to wash my hands?"

He said, very in-charge and knowing-it-all, "Yes! Because you need to learn how to wash!"

"Okay," I answered and went with him over to the sink. This five-year-old boy child would not touch me. All the other kids were standing around, watching, curious. Maybe the thought also had occurred to them that I was dirty; maybe it hadn't. Perhaps they didn't care. But now we were into a science lesson, and that's my favorite subject!

The young student took a cloth and started washing my hands. He changed to a brush when the "dirt" wouldn't come off. He literally scrubbed and scrubbed and scrubbed. He was scrubbing so determinately that I was thinking, *I'm going to start bleeding pretty soon.*

And finally, he looked at my hand and then at my face and resignedly said, "This isn't coming off!"

I said, "No, it doesn't."

He asked, "How come?"

I sat him down in front of me, made room for the other kids in the circle, and explained, "There are some people in the world that have a skin tone that is darker than other people." I remember this conversation like I had it yesterday; that's how impactful it was.

He looked at me and asked, "Is this what happens when you stay in the sun too long?"

I said, "No, if you stay in the sun, you'll get darker, but you won't get this dark." And, I continued, "There are other people who are darker than me."

His eyes opened wide, and he looked like a cartoon with eyes boing-boing-boing all over the place. And now the other kids were jumping in. "What??? People get darker than you???"

The teacher in this classroom was smart enough to grab the globe, and we started to talk in class about Africa and the parts of the skin and how various ethnicities have different skin colors. The teacher found additional materials, and together we created a teachable experience. We also talked about what makes blue eyes and green eyes. A student in the class was native American, and the kids pointed out that he had darker skin. The classroom teacher had calmed down, and most wisely, used this whole incident as the basis for some lessons, and I wound up with a stellar evaluation!

REMARKABLE LEADERSHIP LESSONS

- **People don't know what they don't know.** We assume others experience life just like us… from our perspective. That's not true. Two people can see the same thing and based upon their history/previous experiences, will internalize the experience differently. They will respond differently and expect others to respond as they do. Sometimes you have to demonstrate or explain to help them understand. Learning how to offer your perspective without an attitude of superiority changes how people accept you.

- **How we react to the unexpected is a pivotal moment for those around us.** These are the teachable moments leadership offers.

- **Lessons and wisdom come from the most unlikely places.** Being open to learning and accepting that what you know is not ALL there is to know, can bring you great insights.

UNIVERSAL REMARKABLE LEADERSHIP LESSONS

To set the tone for our time together, here are my universal leadership lessons that will relate to the anecdotes, case histories, and stories throughout the book. You can use/refer back to these leadership lessons throughout your career and as you interact with people around you.

- **Passion Drives Us.** Some will tell you that all you have to do is find the one big passion that drives you, and you'll find your true calling. Others believe our passion develops over time, and we find it not in what we do, but in how our skills contribute to helping others. Passion is that energy, that joy, that desire we feel when our work aligns with what motivates us. Passion is an energy—not a profile, not a skill. For yourself… think about what gets you charged up for the day. What comes easily to you and brings you great satisfaction? What is it that makes people ask, "How did you do that?" and you are genuinely puzzled that they think it's so hard? Look for that thing you do so well and easily in your business, home, family, life… that's your gift or gifts. How can you carry "that" across those boundaries? Only when you acknowledge and honor your gift(s) will you find your passion.
- **Motivation Propels Organization Success.** A simple statement, yet it's so hard to identify what motivates, and then to figure out how to use the motivation as the engine for business success. Executives and management are trained to take outcomes (what they see as results in the status reports they review) and back it out to what they think happened. You can never capture the innate potential of your team when performance is based upon the individual and rewarded with money (assuming that one can motivate someone with a money scorecard).

In continually doing so, executives miss identifying what really drives someone to achieve and make an impact: what keeps someone loyal to an organization. They never capture the power of collective effort.

- No organization runs on the efforts of one person alone. Every organization is by definition the collective and coordinated efforts of everyone to achieve a common goal. What inspires people to do better on their job, to think creatively and go the extra step simply because they want to make a difference? How do you motivate the people around you to voluntarily work together for a common goal? How do you recognize people who go above and beyond and those who work quietly to avoid problems and catastrophes? These are fundamental questions that need to be answered if you are interested in motivating your organization.

- **Valuing Talent.** Management often talks about bringing in top talent but then has a difficult time making those people feel valued. The tendency is to teach. Teaching is imparting knowledge. However, in a world of likes, clicks, and shares, what motivates people may be the thing that get them recognition. In that world, it is more likely that you will get the performance you seek from your team when you provide recognition and "likes" for the behaviors and actions you want to encourage. Do you have a nonfinancial recognition program/process in your organization? How do you personally "like" and "share" someone's achievements? What is the definition of talent? Does it include those who have an expertise and those who enable others to perform? Are your recognition programs pitting how someone describes what was accomplished against how it was done?

- **Strategic Communication.** Remarkable leaders are more strategic with how they communicate with people. Whether they're talking with their leadership, subordinates, or peers, there are four things they do well:

1. **Vision:** To see and describe a future end state and identify the right things to do to get there.
2. **Resource Management:** Ability to obtain, prioritize, delegate responsibility, and take ownership to complete the assignment. When delegating, making sure you've provided the resources needed to complete the project: time, money, people, technology, etc.
3. **Processes to Follow-up:** Follow-up gets clunky at times if it is only around what is urgent or broken as opposed to the strategic point of view. Look at what it is that this person does well and whether you are using their skills in a way that helps keep everyone focused on delivering the vision and outcome desired.
4. **Follow Through:** Ensure that what is planned and scheduled is enacted and completed.

If these four things are not managed, it shows up in the reports from HR, employee engagement surveys, and exit interviews.

COACHING AND LEADERSHIP

"Why is HR included in your book?" some of my early readers asked. In my experience, Human Resource (HR) departments have been relegated to a side function in most companies. The primary job of HR has been to create and implement processes around interviewing/hiring/firing, to administer benefits, and to keep the company free of lawsuits through compliance. Since HR is actually responsible for the structure and systematic way you treat people, it defines your culture. In organizations where HR is thought of as only the way to bring in or exit employees, those corporate cultures don't achieve high performance.

When executives find themselves needing to coach and mentor people and they reach out to HR, there needs to be a way for HR to provide support. Aside from HR professionals being asked to resolve conflicts, HR would benefit from having freelance coaches available to guide employees/executives through a variety of individual situations, because a garden-fresh, outside perspective, can bring light to something that is difficult to see for those with close involvement.

When in a position of authority or you would like to be perceived as a leader, it is not easy to share every thought and "crazy" idea with the people you lead or want to impress. This can make people feel isolated, working in their own silo. Working with someone external allows the freedom of no-conflict, (no one to claim your idea as their own) as well as ensuring confidentiality. What you say in Vegas, stays in Vegas kind of idea. You can risk sharing your craziest thought if you feel confident it won't impact your reputation or credibility. And thus, in the process of objectively talking something out, my clients decide on whether it makes sense to share the concept within the organization. Equally important is role-playing all the scenarios on the most effective way to present a new idea to each of the personalities that might be involved. What's the best approach?

In my experience, as humans we often give more credence to our differences than figuring out how we are alike. A coach can question all parties and help one see the commonalities that can bring communication in a relationship to a shared place, versus *I'm the ONLY one with this situation* type thinking.

We can choose to look at any situation and complain about how the other person is not like us, or we can step back and figure out what we share in our humanity and experiences, to bring us together into an amenable working relationship. Fear underpins our decision to believe no other person can really understand our perspective. Once we identify and name the fear, we can make healthier decisions. Ask yourself, when you look at someone else, do you see what's different, or do you seek to find what is common?

The Human Resources department in most organizations does not dive into the interpersonal connections and communication until there is a conflict or concern, and even then, it's about the legal process and procedures. I've spent years in Human Resources trying to blend the humanity of the workforce into the legal and administrative roles of HR.

I believe one reason it is so difficult is because of the role Human Resources plays in the organization. No matter how well-meaning HR professionals are, everyone they speak to knows, consciously or unconsciously, that their employment life is affected by this person. HR sits in on, or influences most career discussions from salary increases, promotions, and assignments, to who gets hired and who is laid off or terminated. Consequently, no matter how nice they are as a person, trust, vulnerability, and openness only goes so far. The result is every employee is keenly aware that they must appear competent and worthy of continued favor and employment when dealing with HR.

Wise HR professionals don't run from this fact. Instead, they convince others that the best course of action is to quietly find someone outside the organization who can bring the fresh perspective needed to identify the root cause of a problem and implement a sustainable solution.

TWO SIDES TO ANY STORY

One of the challenges I face in writing this book, is that I am writing from my own perspective, just as you lead from your own experiences and outlook. As a woman born and raised without much in terms of financial resources, in a metropolitan city, a person of color and small stature, and who has faced incidents of classism, racism, misogyny (intended and unintended), I am sharing my story, which is likely very different from your story. My role models were likely different from yours. Men and women are treated differently in the world and have different expectations put on us by our families, neighbors, and business associates. What parts of that do you bring into being a leader in the workplace?

Applying what I learned coming up in the world, helped me to become the go-to person in Human Resources of the Fortune 500 companies for which I worked, and then as a leader in coaching for individuals who wanted to achieve their goals. I love working behind the scenes to help remarkable people become extraordinary and satisfied with their own success.

The personal stories I share appear here because they led me to learn something that opened me up, helped me be my best me, now. There are things in your past that you will likely find in common with my story, even if we did not start from the same place. I bring my responsiveness to the workplace, to all Human Resource interactions, and to my coaching clients for them to improve their connections with subordinates, supervisors, and coworkers. My goal is to share how I got there through my story as well as anecdotes from various clients, so you can choose whether you want to follow that path.

As someone who considers him or herself to be enlightened and open to all kinds of people, you might find that my perspective triggers a reaction in you. That's okay. The question is, are you going to shut down your desire to read on, or are you going to notice the reaction and realize that you might have that same response when working with someone who might cause you to shut down then too? What was your goal in choosing to avoid that discussion or ask a question that may make you look a bit naïve, foolish, or imperfect? How does that affect future opportunities for your department or company?

As you read each story, ask yourself:

- What happens to our ability to achieve more if each small interaction and unintentional trigger causes everyone to back away, or reject everything out of pocket from another person without real cause?

• Can I use what triggered me to work on healing, let go of something that just ain't so anymore or something that stops me from growing?

After reading a draft of this book, Bill shared with me: "I have often felt embarrassed by the arrogance and lack of respect for others [from the elders in my family to those] outside of their group…. Thank you for showing me something within myself that is a point of agony that I can now bring to the forefront and heal."

Anthony, another one of my early readers, shared that he was feeling fearful, angry, and challenged when leading a top liquor organization sales team and found himself blaming everyone else when things didn't go as planned. He came to a realization that he would be happier if he achieved the L4 philosophy of integrity and accountability, learning and loving life's lessons. After years of struggling to make an impact in day-to-day interactions, Anthony recognized that the difference had to come from within himself, rather than from changing others. "This lesson led to a better life, one without negative energy but one filled with happiness and joy."

Anthony was raised in a home where slang words based on stereotypes, were used for describing and insulting people. When he read the draft of this book, he remembered a time in his school days when he inadvertently called someone across the room by a derogatory name only to watch the horror in the eyes of his best friend. Anthony never forgot that look. He learned he had to "take off the coat he was wearing if wearing that coat hurt other people." He brought that lesson from childhood into his management role to engage and motivate his diverse sales team and ultimately achieved remarkable, award-winning results. Reading other people's stories, hearing other people's experiences, can help people shed the coats they leave the house wearing, and that might inadvertently hurt others.

The Leadership Lesson I hope you take away from your responses to the stories herein is: Don't get angry or defensive—be reflective.

HOW THIS BOOK REALLY WORKS

This book contains portions of actual case histories. The people in the stories represent a variety of backgrounds. You will likely recognize some of the characteristics or situations from your own experiences. The goal of this book is to provide tools for you to use, as you inspire others (whether your boss, co-workers, and/or direct reports) to higher levels of trust in order to achieve the desired outcomes. The communication strategies I've helped clients to employ have enabled them to create harmonious, productive work environments. Isn't that the ultimate goal of any leader?

HR (and many executives), feels that any situation that involves people needs to involve HR. However, many of these case histories demonstrate that the work of communication on a one-to-one basis happens outside of the HR department. I offer some tips for HR throughout, but much of this is about how you, as a leader, can achieve results.

As you can imagine, confidentiality is essential, and all the stories have been altered in name and in other ways to preserve the anonymity of my clients. In telling their stories, I've attempted to preserve the essence of their experiences, fears, frustrations, sentiments, and words as best as I can. For the majority of the people you'll read about, these stories do not reflect the totality of our time together. Every story is a slice of the time we worked together. On average, I work with my clients for about eighteen months, depending on their specific goals. Work involving reinventing a business culture takes several years.

The point is that behavioral change seldom happens in an instant. Please don't fall into the trap of thinking real, lasting change, happens without effort and attention. Achieving clarity on a situation may happen suddenly, but the work of achieving lasting results—changing habits and thought patterns that don't serve you any longer—well, that takes dedication to a set of skills you hone over time.

Working with executives as an advisor, trainer, and coach, is a very personal and highly interactive experience. To put onto paper what transpires between two people in a room or over a phone line is not easy. And yet, that's what I'm aiming for here. A conversation between me and you to help you determine what you need to know right now to make your next decision. And perhaps you'll come back and read this again when your next big move needs to be made and see the same writings with a new perspective to guide you then too.

The drama is real. The frustration and confusion are real. The pain is definitely real. But as I review the stories as a dispassionate reader in hindsight, it seems all too easy to solve the problem. I can assure you it is not. I can tell you that each person would see a glimmer of clarity and then it would disappear. The same lessons would show up differently and resistance to change would pop up. Procrastination would come in the form of a new opportunity or something more urgent on the "to-do" list. Then just as quickly, they would try one of the lessons in this book, and POW! Success! We'd move one more step towards their goal. They would independently learn how to recognize and address the situation before it got out of hand. We could celebrate a blessing and the joy a new lesson learned brings, and then move on to the next level.

My clients tell me I talk them off the ledge. I can tell you sometimes they were angry with me, frustrated with the growth process at times, and for some—usually just before a real breakthrough—they would hang up the phone on me… doubting the strategies and recommendations.

Then all the pieces would fall into place and they got the job, the raise, the promotion, or the project they wanted. That pesky coworker, boss, or peer would become someone they could work with minus the irritation, anger, or the need to throw up every time they came into the room. Their performance, and the performance of those around them, oftentimes improved.

I tell you… I loved working in the corporate business space. I have spent a lot of time learning how groups of people work together to get stuff done. I have studied what causes one person to be a leader and another equally capable, (sometimes more capable) to not step up.

I have worked in the human performance and effectiveness space almost all of my life. I've studied and practiced the art of leading, coaching, mentoring, and understanding how one's personality and temperament determines choices, reactions, and results.

You see, my gift is hearing what people want and identifying what gets in the way. I've become a better listener by practicing to "hear" the unspoken, and the "all too real" reasons why a group, individual, or business is missing the mark.

What I've learned is that we are all leaders. Every day we influence others—our mere presence influences others. What we forget is every encounter is an opportunity to meet a higher calling, and to be of service to self and others. No one wakes up with the intention of failing to meet our destiny. What we have to offer; our presence, skills, talents, and abilities contributes in a meaningful way. What we want most is for others to see and acknowledge that we matter.

This book is called *Remarkable Leadership Lessons* in part because my clients love quoting my sayings and stories. Remarkable means being worthy of observation and sharing. I am humbled that they encouraged me to share my wisdom with others as I am continually sharing the wisdom of those who taught me.

HOW TO USE THIS BOOK

You can read this book from start to finish or choose to skip around and learn something from each of the individual stories and sections.

- The first section contains stories that will show you how to become a change leader, focused on individual growth.
- The second section comprises stories about understanding mindset, background, and culture: how to go from a Me to a We organization.
- The third section covers how you can impactfully influence others.
- The last section encompasses stories and ideas for leaders/ Human Resource professionals to use to design better organizations or leadership training experiences.
- The addendum will point HR professionals to specific examples that might be useful in coaching employees going through communication challenges.

"*Chicken Soup for the Soul* for business leaders" is how one of my former clients described this book. My hope is that reading even a small section of this book will show you that being a good leader is just one conversation away.

Thanks for joining me.

SETTING THE STAGE: THE FUNDAMENTALS

IDEAS  ACTION

WHERE SELF HELP GOES WRONG

DENISEism:
"It ain't what you don't know that gets you
into trouble. It's what you know for sure
that just ain't so."

Paraphrasing Mark Twain

You may have heard about the 10,000-hour rule. Malcom Gladwell wrote a book called *Outliers* that popularized the idea that it takes about 10,000 hours of practice to master anything. Like many popular ideas, it makes sense on the surface, but fully fleshed out, it is a bit inaccurate.

You may ask, "If it's inaccurate, then how could it be quoted so often?" Good question. The answer is that it's catchy, and it works on accepted premises. So, maybe his book isn't IN-accurate, but it isn't the complete story.

Imagine being a golfer practicing your swing daily. However, every time you hit the ball it veers right. What you're doing is called "slicing" the ball. Then one day you think, *If I turn my body left, then the ball will go where I want it to go.* Sure enough, after several weeks of practice, you've learned how to compensate for a poor stroke.

What you've done is master a poor stroking technique; you haven't become a better golfer.

In that same vein, being a leader isn't something we excel at immediately. It takes education, skill development, and practice. I've held leadership positions and learned that to be a good leader, you have to practice the art of leadership just like you have to practice golf to be a good golfer.

REMARKABLE LEADERSHIP LESSONS

- **For us to remember something, it has to be simple.** Making complex ideas simple, gives our brain a way to organize and categorize information.
- **Simple is catchy.** The premise that spending 10,000 hours practicing something will make one a master is appealing, easy to understand, and repeatable.
- **It lines up with what we already know to be true.** It is true that to master anything you have practice, and I mean practice a lot. The problem is most of us practice poorly (often permanently cementing the wrong thing), or learn shortcuts, causing us to continually practice inaccurately.

POWER OF BELIEF: IDENTIFYING TALENT AND BUILDING THEM UP

FEARING POLITICAL FALLOUT

A moment of insight came when I wanted to hire a REALLY talented African American woman as my Director of HR. She would have been my second in command. When I made a proposal she turned me down, as she did each time I repeated the offer.

I couldn't understand why. I knew she wanted the job. We got along great during the interview process, so I was baffled as to why she said no. I took her to lunch and asked for her rationale. She explained there would be too much political fallout if there were two African American women in charge. No white company could take it and ultimately, she feared they would turn against us.

I asked, "So you turned down a good position because you are afraid that too many black people would be working together?" She said yes. I leaned forward, looked her straight in the eye, and in a low, deliberate tone said, "I wish someone would say they were uncomfortable or thought it was a problem that I hired too many black people. My answer would be: when it is a problem that we are hiring too many white people, then we can talk. But until then, there is no problem; there is nothing else to discuss."

She grinned, leaned in towards me, and said with finality, "I'll take the job."

REMARKABLE LEADERSHIP LESSONS

Too often we are defined by our limitations and how others do things. Helping others find the strength and abilities to succeed within themselves is the most important leverage leaders/executives have for unleashing untapped performance.

- **The purpose of inspiration is to offer you an opportunity** to achieve and move beyond your limiting beliefs. The rest is up to you.

- **Nothing changes until you have the courage to do something different, something out of your comfort zone.** The conversation in your head talks about why not, the consequences of stepping out, what could happen, and why now is or isn't the right time.

- **Too much head talk makes complacency comfortable.** Complacency makes fear comfortable and acceptable.

WHY WE FAIL TO ACHIEVE HIGHER LEVELS OF PERFORMANCE

DENISEism:
We Are All Leaders. Skilled leaders teach with
intention; Everyone else leads accidentally.

Stop and think through the job of a leader at its most basic level. We teach each other how to be with each other and what to expect.

Leading and influencing others carries great responsibility and risks, which is why so many people shy away from leading. It is far less risky to focus on the labor of your hands than how smart we are; thus, we stay silent, letting someone else make the big decisions.

Stepping up to the leadership plate means risking criticism. Steppi3ng up to lead often means stepping outside the authority vested by your position and putting yourself out there to hear the opinions (or criticisms) of others. And let's face it, although some opinions matter more to us than others, all criticism stings.

Workplaces are built on a hierarchy of talent and leaders. This creates a false platform of safety. There are those who are authorized to make decisions, while others are there to execute those decisions. Those who make policies are deemed more important, more influential.

People expect the Human Resource department to lead, define, set, and manage the culture. The truth is that Human Resources is responsible for codifying the culture; it is everyone else who defines and makes it real.

VISION FOR HR

I think the Human Resource (HR) function is at a turning point. It's time HR professionals make the decision to show up in a new and different way. To stop talking about being invited to the table. I see us setting the agenda at the table, or even creating our own table where decisions about people, products, services, and performance impacts are made.

I firmly believe that those who choose to enter HR as a profession, must understand that the collective work of nation building, creating community, and ensuring equality, is not just an idea, but something we manage every day.

It is through our work—whatever our role—that we gain meaning and create value in our lives. Too many people are unable to see and embrace the larger concepts and overidentify with work as their entirety of value. We should come from a belief system of being worthy because you exist. Work is what we do, not who we are.

We view workplaces as marketplaces where a person's job title and amount of money earned dictates status and rank. We have forgotten that no work produced is less valuable than any other, that we all are puzzle pieces required to fit together to complete the whole.

Today, many HR executives compete with other departments for funding based upon a rational model that says people act logically and in their own best interest, and yet, people don't act rationally and in their own best interest. We buy lottery tickets in hopes of getting the winning number, all the while knowing that the chances of winning are slim to none. We buy clothes from designers when we can get the same functionality from cheaper stores. Marketers know this.

Marketers know that how you present the product/concept is every bit as important as the item being sold, if not more so. Leadership is fundamentally about marketing and selling an idea. One that people just have to have.

REMARKABLE LEADERSHIP LESSONS

- Ask Yourself… whether as an executive, manager, or HR professional…
  - What's the idea you are collectively selling?
  - Who creates the strategy and ensures it gets implemented?
  - Who understands how to get the best out of your people?
  - Does everyone understand their role?
  - How do you treat boundary breakers?

The answers to these questions send quiet messages to everyone in the organization about what's important, what gets rewarded, and what doesn't.

- If you then asked ten people in your organization to answer these same questions, what would they say, and what would be the pattern that emerges from their collective response?

Whatever it is, these are the stories that drive and underpin performance in your company, department, or workgroup.

SECTION I
CHANGE IS DIFFICULT...
BECOMING A CHANGE LEADER

"The road of life is strewn with the bodies of promising people. People who show promise yet lack the confidence to act."

Iyanla Vanzant

IDEAS  ACTION

PROFILE: PREPARING FOR THE C-SUITE CHALLENGE

DENISEism:
Polishing a diamond takes finesse,
not brute force.

S tanding at the sink in the ladies' room, Imani turned her head from side to side to assure that her impeccably coifed black hair was in place, checked her perfectly aligned, bright white teeth for a stray lipstick smudge, and then pushed back her shoulders and stretched to her full 5'8" frame. She was confident that she was wearing just enough make-up to look sophisticated, polished, and professional, but not too much. Her ensemble, selected and reviewed and amended for the past three days, was conservative banker chic.

The statement pieces in her ears, on her fingers, around her neck, said: "I'm at the top of my game!" The meeting she was about to walk into was THE meeting of her career to date. She was finally entering the Board Room—the C-Suite challenge.

For several years, the word around the organization was that careers were made or destroyed based upon how well you stood up to the scrutiny from the most senior executives. Legend had it this was the make-it or break-it presentation of her life (or at least for her eleven-year career at this bank.)

As Imani walked the hallway toward the board room foyer, she started running through everything we had discussed in preparation for this very moment.

- **Confidence**—you're prepared and you've earned the right to be here based on quantifiable results delivered for years.
- **Body language**—project a self-assured posture. Presence matters. It can work for you or against you.
- **Provide answers** to the posed questions by being **direct, but not challenging. Be succinct.**
- **Breathe.** It keeps the brain engaged and minimizes the impact of fear on thinking.
- **Listen** to the questions. **Take time** to formulate an answer. **Speak clearly** and make sure to **look at everyone** as you answer.

The assistant welcomed Imani to enter, and Imani went through the double doors with a silent exhale as a smile illuminated her face. It was the same smile she shared with Oprah and Ava Duvernay at an event weeks before, and as she and her successful businessman husband circumnavigated the room at the exclusive *Essence* magazine party in New Orleans, and at all the fundraising events at home. Years of experience taught Imani how to work a room, and thanks to our sessions, she was confident that this was going to be a successful presentation.

A few hours later, a relieved Imani was excitedly telling me, "It went so well! I answered every question and didn't hesitate or get stumped. The CEO said as I was leaving, 'Imani, you've set the bar pretty high for anyone else in that chair!'"

"Can you believe it?" Imani exclaimed. "Isn't that wonderful? I'm still shaking. It was amazing. I couldn't have gotten through this so well without all the work we did. Thank you, thank you!"

After the C-suite meeting, the execs called Imani's boss, Nancy, and told her that Imani was impressive, and to make sure Imani wasn't at risk of leaving.

PERSONAL BRANDING

Three months before the C-Suite challenge, Imani and I first began working together. Imani had attended a leadership development workshop, where she was informed by "everyone!" that she needed to have and own a personal brand.

Imani questioned "everyone" extensively. Asking questions like why she needed a "personal brand statement," and what could it be? What was the best way to start thinking about creating a brand statement? Even with Imani's keen analytical skills, she left the workshop with no idea on how to do it. Everything she offered the group was met with less than positive feedback.

Nancy, Imani's mentor, was a capable and politically savvy black woman who successfully made it to the senior executive levels in a male-dominated world. After hearing the feedback from the women's leadership workshop, she knew Imani needed more than the typical leadership training programs could offer. Nancy decided to hire a coach for Imani out of her budget after talking with the head of HR. There was one critical stipulation… No one could know.

Nancy knew the culture at the company very well. It was highly competitive, and paying for an outside coach could be exploited as having an unfair advantage by others who wanted to move up into senior leadership. It is a tag that women, and people of color carry, especially in competitive environments.

Nancy shared with me that she wanted Imani to learn how to take bigger, bolder, and measured risks. To ascend into the C-suite, Imani had to learn to present and define ideas that would increase the competitive positioning of the organization. Imani had to display the kind of executive presence that signaled her resolve, ability, and thought-leadership.

Entering Imani's office on the 18th floor of the building, I noticed the vast windows that let in the afternoon light. At our first meeting, Imani came from around her big desk, passing a wall of bookcases with awards, plaques, and magazine articles on display. When I commented on the impressive collection, Imani quickly dismissed the comment, saying it was displayed to show people her level of experience. It's just a "power display," she sheepishly admitted.

IMANI'S STORY

Before a coach can offer feedback and reflections, you have to understand a clients' history. What happened to them that taught them to see, think, and believe in their point of view.

In this case, Imani described herself as growing up "dirt poor" in a two-parent family. She earned a scholarship to Greg Morris University and planned a future in economics. Imani told me that all she ever wanted to do was to help others get out of poverty. She firmly believed a good education was the differentiating factor for her.

Imani's a thriver, much more than a survivor. As she tells her life story, it is clear that what others would call adversity was (in Imani's mind) just what you had to do to succeed. It had not been an easy route, but she got tough enough, and hardened up. From adversity, diamonds are created.

In asking Imani for her definition of effective leadership, she talked about the desire to be part of a team, to be cooperative and collaborative, and work towards the greater good for all. "Right now, the company wants us to improve our engagement scores. The most important feedback I hear from my direct reports is about the workload. I have to find a way to rebalance the workload, but our company is so cost-conscious."

Senior management wanting more and more without providing additional headcount, is a common complaint from every executive, in every company. Do more with less. I listened intently to Imani, wondering if this organization knew when it would hit the breaking point. I found myself silently questioning how anyone in Imani's role would know they were at the breaking point before it costs too much.

REMARKABLE LEADERSHIP CONCEPT IN ACTION: WHEN CUTTING COSTS GOES TOO FAR

Over and over, the refrain to do more with less in corporations has led to unintended consequences. Two in particular....

- **Loss of the most prized talent.** As jobs have changed, competition for talent has increased. Passive candidates, those individuals who aren't actively looking for a job but are known for their ability to deliver, are sought after and heavily courted. These individuals have nurtured their skills and become highly efficient at delivering on organizational objectives. In the world of sports, these individuals are known as free agents. In business, when a company's cost cutting makes it difficult to reach objectives or reduces the ability to retain a support team, it gives free agents an incentive to move to positions where the work is both interesting and utilizes their strengths.
- **Erosion of trust.** Trust is a critical component in every workplace. Without it, managers have to work three times as hard because employees are unclear and confused about what matters. It's an inconsistent message for senior executives to say employee engagement matters and then cut costs by eliminating headcount and not addressing how the work gets done. The message internalized is, "we only matter as cogs in the wheel for you to get a big bonus."

When someone is fully engaged in surviving, every new opportunity brings doubts and second-guessing to the forefront.

Thus, whenever a new position became available and people in Imani's organization badgered her to apply, she took a pause. Her hesitation allowed her to envision herself in a new role and confirm internally that she wanted to do the work to succeed at a higher level. Her core battle was the thought that if she didn't do well, then she would be let go in the next round of cost-cutting. As the primary breadwinner for her family (both her own and extended family) taking on any new position was risky. Imani would think: "I'm safe, right where I am. I can do this job well. Why take the risk?"

This risk-assessment moment, this time to fully consider taking on a new role or additional responsibilities, is not uncommon for many women, people caring for loved ones with illness or challenges, people of color, or anyone outside the majority in an organization to have.

For Imani, it was a pattern repeated throughout her career. Imani agonized over every new opportunity presented to her. Her promotions came as a result of someone urging her to apply rather than applying because she knew she was qualified, or from personal ambition. And yet, her record speaks for itself. Imani successfully worked her way up from day-to-day operations to Vice President of Economic Development. The company paid for her to attend a two-year certificate program at the Wharton School for Leadership. It was apparent to me that others, both inside and outside the bank, believed Imani was a highly talented, highly valued person they wanted to retain.

As they continued to talk, I noted that Imani could easily quote her "big bangs." One success after another achieved over the last few years. Imani snapped her fingers—click, click, click—as she talked about her strategy and how she went about implementing it. As self-aware as Imani seemed, she didn't believe she had a unique or valuable skill set.

"What do you think is valuable or special?" I asked her.

"If I bring in $500,000,000 deal," answered Imani.

"But," I pointed out, "over here, you closed a $400,000,000 deal." Imani humbly replied, "It's not like I did it alone. It was a team effort. Now, if I could personally deliver that deal as Nancy does... She makes one or two phone calls, and it happens. Leading the team is just what I'm supposed to do."

REMARKABLE LEADERSHIP MINDSET:
THE DOWNSIDE OF THE "WE" APPROACH

Having a "we did it" mindset is the hallmark of highly skilled executives. However, for women, there's a downside. How others know about you and what you do is dependent on how you speak about what you do. The subtle difference between women and men possessing a "We" mindset is the art of leadership. Men intuitively know every team has a leader who sets the vision, helps clarify the objectives and delegates responsibility, follows up, and ensures follow-through on agreements. Women may know this fact but focus too much on collaboration and sharing credit. Their language leads others to believe they were not in charge.

This soft, indirect type of conversation is used quite often by women. In early career management roles, recognition comes from implementing the priorities of others. At the senior executive level, you set the vision, clarify the objectives, and delegate goals and execution to lower-level managers.

Imani had the ear of her business-savvy husband to discuss the pros and cons of all prospective moves. If a decision did not turn out to be the right one, Imani knew her husband was there for her and that they would examine and discuss the options and consequences together. Not everyone has that built-in resource.

Building a support network is critical to getting through tough decision-making moments. Like any corporation with a Board of Directors, like the White House Cabinet of experts meant to support the President, you need objective voices to offer insights on how you are showing up and to work through the pros and cons of major decisions. You are the CEO of your life at all times. Successful CEOs have built a network of advisors from tops in the field, whose advice and critical thinking ability raises the likelihood of good outcomes.

REMARKABLE LEADERSHIP LESSON: CREATING A LEADERSHIP CABINET

The function of your personal leadership cabinet is to expand your perspective or knowledge on a situation, highlight the strengths and weaknesses of various options, and provide counsel. Your cabinet can advise you on how to use your unique combination of skills and perspectives to approach a situation.

Your informal cabinet might meet over drinks at a lounge, brunch at the house, lunch in a restaurant, via telephone or video conference, or simply through emails. It does not need to have a formal structure nor do all the members need to gather at once, nor do any of the members even need to know that there IS a cabinet!

Who might you include in your cabinet?

- a paid coach
- family members with good strategic mindsets (watch out for emotional baggage and "how your decision impacts me" positioning)
- friends
- spouse
- mentors
- networking support group members
- chamber of commerce members
- former coworkers or bosses
- current or former instructors/teachers
- trade group roundtable participants

- speakers from conferences outside your core expertise
- authors of books (read the book and learn, or join the author's Facebook group to ask for feedback)

You most likely have a cabinet already but didn't realize you could maximize their contributions by thinking of them in a more formal way, and structuring your questions to each to get a consensus of options and opinions from which to choose.

THERE ARE TWO TYPES OF LEADERS— STRATEGISTS AND VISIONARIES

Imani didn't understand the difference between sitting in the C-Suite office and every other executive position. She was unclear about the difference between strategic versus visionary leadership.

REMARKABLE LEADERSHIP MINDSET: VISION VS. STRATEGY

Effective senior executives are skilled at seeing many possibilities to improve results. The challenge with seeing many options is there are too many good ones. Strategies don't fail because of a lack of opportunities; they fail because executives can't pick one and stick with it. Experienced senior executives succeed because they make tough choices on what results to achieve. After that, it's managing focus and resources to achieve the vision or desired outcomes.

Strategic Leadership:

Strategists' select safe, proven, and incremental improvements. Strategists' sell the idea of certainty, predictability, and control. They are great at improving the current strategy.

Visionary Leadership:

Visionaries see how continuing to do the same things will eventually lead to a plateau at best and a downfall at worst. Visionaries are able to keep an eye outward towards the market, constantly looking for and sensing when changes that matter are on the horizon. We live in uncertain, complex, and volatile times. Visionaries are needed to see what others don't and help organizations—people—adapt to what's coming. They make decisions that ensure the organization is developing the capabilities for tomorrow while doing what needs to be done today, based on the organization's unique capabilities.

A picture was forming in my mind. Here Imani was, being exposed to other visionary leaders, including Nancy (her boss). They advised her on various aspects of leadership, influence, and power by telling her what to do. What she, like so many of my clients needed, was to learn how to be both strategic and visionary at the same time. She needed a roadmap on what, how, and when to prepare others and push for change.

Imani's boss (and others) was asking her to step up, to stand out, to show that she could become a visionary leader. A creator. Imani was being cultivated to have a more significant impact on the lives of others. Imani worried… the regional presidents (primarily white males), weren't being asked to make bold, visibly risky decisions, so why was she? To move out of an implementer role and more into leadership, Imani was being asked to reach beyond her comfort zone, which felt risky. Growing up as she did and climbing the ladder in an unfamiliar world, Imani couldn't help but question if her bosses were setting her up to fail, or were they preparing her to move higher up in the organization?

According to the research that Imani knew very well, women and people of color in corporate America usually find it much more challenging to bounce back after a failure. White men could historically fail and still land on their feet, whereas for a woman of color, getting that next job or assignment is harder. On the other hand, Imani also knew that to make it to the higher levels, people of color, minorities, and women in particular, have to take on riskier projects and assignments than their white male counterparts.

For someone in the majority of an organization with a solid reputation to protect, the act of recommending someone outside of the majority for a project/promotion requires confidence that the person being recommended will not fail. Imani could not reflect poorly on the person taking a risk by recommending her. I explained to Imani that being invited to the C-Suite for the presentation meant that people in authority saw potential in her and wanted to get the buy-in from the others at their level. Imani successfully delivering a compelling story describing a new use of current resources would help those in authority to feel confident in recommending her for bigger and more influential roles in the organization.

Unfortunately, all the advice from well-meaning mentors, advisors, and friends wasn't designed to help Imani understand what she needed to do differently to reassure those leaders that she could meet the new challenges. Most advice-givers believe "If I just tell you, I've helped you." But words don't teach, and they certainly don't create the safety and engender the trust needed to move out of the familiar. Our mind seeks assurances that we'll be safe. Abraham Maslow's work proved that the need for safety, predictability, and control is paramount for each of us. Without it, we are unable to move forward.

I explained to Imani how this fantastic $400 million deal was a testament to her leadership capabilities. "You're the person that, for a year, developed the relationships, formulated an idea that no one had thought of, worked through analytics that culminated in a deal of that size. You are as much a part of the success of that deal as the President who stood in front of the cameras announcing the deal."

Imani responded with, "But I'm just doing my job."

I said, "Yes, and you demonstrated that you could do more. This is what Nancy means when she says think bigger and be bolder. That one act is a clear demonstration of your visionary leadership potential."

I continued, "The issue with moving into a C-Suite level position is that you are working beside guys who know how to speak authoritatively and commandingly about their accomplishments. And if you're not totally convinced that your idea has merit, is workable, and the right direction, you'll lose." Imani had to think about that for a bit.

I asked, "What do you want in the future?"

Imani said she did not see herself in her boss's seat.

When I asked, "What about being the Division President?"

"NO, NO, NO!" Imani shot back, her head shaking.

"Why?" I asked.

"Well, I don't think I'm qualified."

Frustrated, I asked, "So why do you want a coach?"

Imani went back to needing help in creating a personal brand. I initially thought Imani had a will issue, that she just didn't have the will to write good things about herself. But that wasn't the root of the problem. I realized it was a skill issue. Imani's inability to write a "brand statement" that was approachable and authentic about herself lay in her belief system.

She could write a resume in corporate-speak, but couldn't see herself as the architect of her destiny. For years, she held on to the idea that whatever she achieved wasn't enough and could be tossed aside at any moment, and she would be out of a job.

Imani already had an established brand within her company and in the community that was known, trusted, and valued. When I asked her what others would say about her, she was quick to answer, "I get things done and work with people to make sure the right things get done."

I asked Imani if she wanted to move into a more visionary leadership role, or did she want to continue implementing other people's ideas and programs? When Imani thought about it, she said she wanted to move to the next level. She was ready to share her ideas and help others to implement her vision. She was willing to take on some risk. "Within reason," she backtracked with a laugh.

About six weeks later, Imani created her own personal brand statement.

> *I am creating sustainable communities that break the bonds of poverty by using collaboration, communication, and consistency to change the lives of others for the better.*

She began working on improving educational opportunities in nine states because upon reflection, she acknowledged that it was knowledge/education that had made the difference for her.

REMARKABLE LEADERSHIP MINDSET: DO YOU HAVE C-SUITE POTENTIAL?

Grooming for a C-Suite role means breaking out of the habit of asking for permission. You're in the room because you've already demonstrated that you can chart a safe course. You have to develop an action plan, confidently point out the risks, explain how you'll mitigate them, and describe the rewards they'll see if you succeed.

This higher level in any organization requires a person to demonstrate readiness for battle and capability for presenting alternative futures, revisions to existing status quo, and to defend those possibilities against naysayers. It requires the ability to influence others to step out of the crowded field for a reward that is not necessarily guaranteed.

WE TEACH OTHERS HOW TO BE WITH US

Over the next eight months, I helped Imani focus on understanding how to have great conversations that caused her team of Vice Presidents and Directors to self-identify strategies and fund programs in states.

By changing the way Imani held staff meetings, pushing her team to set a higher bar and to take on more of the work Imani was doing, (to her pleasant surprise) performance improved for several of her lowest performers without drama.

The new format for her staff meetings included:

- Sending out emails in advance to set the stage, which included:
  - Shared expectations of what would/should come out of the meetings.
  - Key decision points to be discussed.
  - A list of answers that needed to be collected by the end of the meeting.
- Sharing with the group an aggregate of all the individual reports she sees.
  - Breaking out the high, medium, and low performance stats with no names, gave people a way to see how they ranked relative to their peers because they knew their own numbers. It was a way to avoid public shame or embarrassment.
  - Instead of telling them what to do, Imani asked, *"What would it take for all of us to get to the next level?"*
  - Imani held discussions on how to improve key processes and cash flow so their department would improve the performance of other parts of the business dependent on them.

The result of this revised team meeting structure improved performance overall. Bottom performers came to Imani to thank her for not calling them out. Feeling supported instead of embarrassed, they were more transparent about their struggles. As part of her plan, Imani reduced giving advice and direction and asked them more questions. Doing so improved their ability to think more critically and broadly about their work.

Imani and I worked together to change Nancy's mind too. Although Nancy wanted and encouraged Imani to make more decisions, she was caught off guard when Imani was prepared to defend her position steadfastly (a new behavior). When you change, others will either allow you to change or try to put you back in the box. If unprepared, it's easy to give up and go back to what worked previously. In our work together, Imani and I devised a strategy for responding to Nancy's resistance. Imani reminded Nancy that part of the professional growth skills she learned in coaching included presenting ideas with conviction, and then Imani went on to emphasize the proof that the new moves would work out.

One conversation or meeting won't change a person's mind. Let's face it… we all feel overwhelmed, overworked, underappreciated, occasionally pissed off, and sure we've been pissed on. Maybe that's true. But, more often than not, it isn't. Changing our mind means changing our point of view. What would be different if that person who was criticizing you or blocking your idea wasn't the enemy? What would it take for you to see challenges as opportunities?

REMARKABLE LEADERSHIP LESSONS

- **The presenting problem is rarely the root cause of a person's discomfort or pain.** Too often well-meaning managers, friends, and family members will tell you what to do. What they are really doing is telling you what they would do based upon their skills, experiences, risk assessment, and the probability of success according to their past experiences. Rarely are they offering advice related to the original question or situation. We improve our ability to perform by reflecting on what we've done, more than by watching or being told by others. For Imani, creating a brand statement was helpful because it was aspirational. It called her to align her beliefs and abilities with a future vision of herself as a servant to others.

- **Recognize what others see in you that you can't see in yourself.** When you hear a compliment or complaint, what's your first reaction? For a split second, do you think that person is kind, mean, or crazy? Imani struggled to figure out what everyone else wanted and what they saw in her because she couldn't see it in herself. Have you ever felt that way?

- **Stepping up when others see you as a leader.** Often, we are blind to the value of our capabilities. As such, we can't grasp what others see in us. Imani was comfortable being led by others because that was her past and how she defined her value. But her supporters saw the potential for her to have a bigger impact. When put in a tough position, facing conflicting and competing priorities, Imani soared. She was able to lead her team, create supporters, keep them motivated, and continue to perform better than the year before. In adverse conditions, she delivered brilliant solutions. Continuing to refine and perfect one's abilities and skills will lead to effective leadership and coaching of others in the organization. The challenge is seeing how we've grown, opening up to let others see our growth, and using what others are saying about us as part of a growth strategy.

**REMARKABLE LEADERSHIP MINDSET:
SKILLS NEEDED TO BE A SUCCESSFUL
SENIOR EXECUTIVE**

- Prove the ability to see what others can't, and then articulate it so others can grasp it.
- Break new concepts down into approachable milestones. Milestones that others can turn into measurable objectives, tasks, and outcomes.
- Build a culture where follow-up is important. Follow-up includes hosting meetings that drive self-directed learning, and...
- Ensure execution continues in such a way that engenders accountability and gives agency for your team to accomplish the necessary work of building a sustainable, growing organization.

THE POWER OF BELIEF

DENISEism:
Change your perspective, change your life.

I remember, from my days at the gas company, when I assembled a team of people to restructure our health costs. The goal of the team was to find a way to reduce the cost of healthcare by $1M. In the end the team achieved a $15M cost savings.

Just before we gained approval for all the changes, I stopped by the desk of one of the women on the team. I was praising her for an idea she had that saved us about $500,000. She was sitting at her desk in a cubicle. As I ended my comment, she looked up at me and asked why I chose her to be on the team. Without thinking, I told her I believed in her and went on to say that I saw she had the smarts and the experience to figure out how to make a difference. I'll never forget her moving response. She said to me in a timid but matter-of-fact way, "No one has ever believed in me like that. You believed in me when I didn't." I responded by sharing with her that what I saw was someone who had been holding back. All she needed was someone to open the door and let out what was already there.

I knew she had the skill and assumed she knew it too. I assumed she knew she was capable and just needed someone to give her an opportunity. That was an assumption on my part. What I learned is that there are two parts to self-confidence. The ability to do (skill) and the belief we can do (will). She didn't believe she could find a way to successfully achieve the goal and reluctantly just showed up because she didn't have a way out—all the while never really believing anything would change.

We assume others see opportunity just like we do. However, most of the time that's not true. Our perspective is just one perspective, and that perspective defines what's possible, probable, and what's not even an option. Change your perspective, change your life.

PROFILE: A SOLUTION FOR IMPOSTER SYNDROME— KNOW THYSELF

Sitting at her home office desk, staring at the resume template open on her laptop screen, Ebony wondered, *What can I even put in here? I ran my own business for twelve years, and it failed. These people I work for now are younger than me, and they don't understand what I'm talking about. I've had lots of jobs; which ones are relevant? The template wants me to write my "skills." What skills? How do I know what to include and what's a waste of space? And how do I answer the big question: What do I even want to do next?*

Ebony switched over to her LinkedIn profile, hoping for inspiration, and realized she needed to update that too. Her page sounded flat, not fresh or genuine. Nothing written on the page expressed who she really felt she was. Nothing seemed relevant. She thought, *Even I wouldn't hire myself based on what's in front of me!*

Ebony presents as a stylish, beautiful, creative, and powerful black woman. Very high energy. A former New Yorker, she has a "get-shit-done" attitude. Her style of communication is direct and to the point. There's little genteel subtlety about it. No pretty soft language that rolls off the tongue in long notes like fresh pasta coming out of the pasta maker, getting there whenever it's done. Adjusting to a Southern pace, the cultural lack of urgency is an on-going challenge.

Having reached the beginnings of middle age but blessed with good genes, she looked years younger. After twelve years of working for herself, she found herself working as a store manager with twenty-somethings in the retail cosmetics world. Over her lifetime, she experienced some rough business and personal situations that left her with a suitcase full of self-doubts. Ebony asked me to help with the new profile and skills assessment as thoughts of leaving her job were entering her mind more frequently.

"What should I include?" Ebony asked me. "I'm ready to make a move… but to what?"

Ebony explained her situation, "The people where I am are idiots! They ignore my ideas, set ridiculous processes in place that I know won't work. I tell them they won't work, but they won't let me fix them, and then, when the processes fail, they blame me. They penalize me for hiring and training young employees who succeed and then move on to better jobs elsewhere. I just don't fit in!"

CONVERSATIONS THAT MOVE US, DERAIL US

I explained the coaching process to Ebony, and scheduled time together to see what it all meant for her future once the data was gathered.

- First, we worked together to identify Ebony's skills and talents using three assessments and discussing the results.
- Then we reviewed her previous work history. We began gathering old resumes, evaluations, and any other feedback from previous supervisors, peers, and direct reports.
- Lastly, we listed the results or outcomes that excited Ebony the most.

REMARKABLE LEADERSHIP TOOLS:
BEHAVIORAL ASSESSMENTS

There was a time that I adamantly disliked the use of personality and behavioral assessments. In my experience as an HR professional responsible for leadership development and nurturing a productive workplace environment, I found the best-case use of assessments more of a novelty, and in the worst cases, the results devastated relationships and harmed the psyche of women and people of color.

It wasn't until I started my business that I understood the usefulness of these assessments. The real value is in who you select to conduct the debrief and how skilled that person is in helping others use them for their benefit.

The easy answer is to use them as part of your hiring and selection process, then deal with the issue of diversity later— and what often happens is you hire people just like you. When markets are stable, the impact can be invisible. Today, markets are unstable and can change in an instant. Without diversity of thought and a well skilled employee base capable of valuing different points of view, senior executives leave their companies vulnerable.

The primary behavioral assessments I use, identifies how a person makes decisions. It identifies what information a person looks for to determine if an option is good or bad. It identifies what the person is most passionate about, what motivates them; it helps them understand how others react to their communication style and lastly, the impact of their presence on others.

Skilled facilitators are able to take that information, teach others how to use their natural skills to perform better, connect and help others perform better, and improve their (or their team's), critical thinking skills. I use it with leaders to help them build the trust necessary to do better problem solving, improve the reaction time of their team, and hold others accountable for actions.

As I went through Ebony's old resumes, I was impressed! Ebony had started and built two different businesses.

Like so many women entrepreneurs, she did everything in her company while taking care of her children. Ebony, a single mother, said her goal was to earn a living and raise her children. One of her children was born with several life-threatening disabilities. Her products were a result of trying alternative therapies to make her child's life better. One business she built was in the skincare industry and the other in the mind, body, and fitness industry. She formulated, manufactured, branded, labeled, and marketed natural skincare products.

The products worked incredibly well, but as we know, having great products doesn't mean you'll have a successful business. Building a team is the key to long-term success and profitability, which Ebony didn't do.

Many small businesses fail because they don't know how to create a cohesive team of people capable of growing the business past the owner's limited abilities. Additionally, because entrepreneurs are birthed from a personal need—driven by an idea and lifestyle desires that don't fit the typical corporate mode—they don't have the advisor network, capital, knowledge, or experience to understand the limitations inherent in running a solo business.

After she finally closed her struggling business, Ebony took a job at a brand-name retailer, leveraging her knowledge of skincare and beauty products. She began as a cosmetic sales associate and quickly moved up to counter and prestige brand manager.

When I met Ebony, she had been recognized as taking a low-performing store off the "troubled" list and turning it into a high-performing store. Job after job showed Ebony's creativity, ingenuity, ability to manage, see problems and solve them, plan, and implement. I couldn't understand how Ebony believed she didn't have any skills to market!

As a next step, I indexed the tasks Ebony had mastered when starting and running two different companies. Ebony needed to see that even though her two companies eventually closed, the expertise gained remained a part of her. Ebony admitted that she was in so much pain after the failure of her second business that she couldn't see anything positive at all.

Ebony's self-confidence grew as I kept pointing out how her experiences led her to mastery. Together we identified all the talents to include in her profile and emphasize in any interviews. Ebony learned the questions to ask at meetings so she would feel in control of her future.

One day Ebony told me, "This whole thing is about me being in charge of my own life, my destiny. I want to know where I'm going. I need your help to believe that it's possible. I've always just believed that I did what I had to do. My focus was on making a good life for me and my children. I've never seen myself through someone else's eyes the way you're talking to me now! I questioned myself often, wondering who would hire me. Now I believe I would hire me!"

Over the next few weeks, we worked on Ebony's elevator pitch: how to describe herself without either bragging or diminishing her value. The key to a good elevator pitch is in its brevity. It feels like small talk. Good ones are about thirty to sixty seconds, and when you're done talking, the other person knows what you do, how you can help them, and how they can help you.

Together, we practiced interviewing to speak confidently about her accomplishments at each job instead of just listing the tasks required and when that job took place. Ebony went from diminishing her value because it's just "what I do to survive," and that's "nothing special" to appreciating herself as someone who could see her ability to command a team, run a department, and succeed as an executive at a company.

One day, Ebony called me. The excitement in her voice was palpable. She had an interview at an organic skincare company.

The website and company reviews talked about corporate commitment to the environment, and their values. The founders were like her; they started the company to make a difference. The interviews went well, and Ebony accepted the offer.

REMARKABLE LEADERSHIP EDGE: CREATING YOUR OWN ELEVATOR PITCH VS. BRAND STATEMENT

You are not a brand if you are an employee. You have a reputation. A brand is a stated promise that doesn't change over time. Tide is a brand. You know instantly what Tide is good for and what it's not. A reputation is how people see you and connect with you. Good or bad, your reputation lets people know how to connect with you, how far to trust you, and how to engage with you. People can manufacture a personal brand. For example, Oprah is a brand. Michael Jordan, Tony Robbins, RuPaul and Jennifer Lopez—all brands. In a brand statement, you are inviting people to hire you for your unique expertise or market appeal. A brand doesn't change, only evolves over time.

An elevator pitch is a brief statement (takes about the length of an elevator ride to deliver) that answers a question or makes an offer. It is a statement, up to about three sentences long, that describes an aspect of you and should be consistent with your reputation. This would be the statement you might use when someone asks a question like, "Tell me about yourself." or "Why should I hire you?" or "What's unique about you?"

Ask yourself a few questions to collect the data you want to consider for your statement. Your goal is to write a simple statement for someone to figure out if they want to engage with you and learn more. You might wind up with multiple statements— (for personal life to help people determine "Do I want to date you?"), family (what to say at that reunion of long-lost relatives or at holiday parties), work/business (hire me for that job I covet), volunteer role (become a board member for a nonprofit you love), etc.

When you have the answers to these questions, begin to write your elevator pitch with action words such as: People tell me my best work always involves me doing... I create, I sustain, I implement...

My elevator pitch is more of a question. "Would you like to lead more effectively? I teach executives the conversational skills that achieve remarkable results."

THE CHALLENGE OF MAKING HIGH PERFORMERS FEEL VALUED, RECOGNIZED, AND REWARDED

DENISEism:
With every accomplishment comes
a new level and a new devil.

About three years later and what seemed like out of the blue, Ebony called me. After a few pleasantries, I asked, "What's up?" Ebony talked extensively about her relationship with her manager. She was hired once again to turn around an underperforming store. At the end of the first year, the store was taken off the corporate target list for closing, but Ebony was struggling to lead the team and work with her manager.

Ebony was different from her floor supervisors and managers. She described them as amiable. They really wanted to be liked and thus tried to avoid conflict or for that matter, any sense of disagreement. As a result, they were uncomfortable with the sales portion of their job.

The supervisor/manager's job is to set and hold others to agreements and boundaries and hold them accountable for their actions.

Yet, amiable personalities aren't comfortable giving critical or developmental feedback. Ebony's district manager, Eve, hired Ebony because she had that needed skill but didn't expect so much push-back from the rest of the store management team. Ebony is not only comfortable offering feedback but is very good at pinpointing what actions or behaviors are needed to achieve efficient, effective sales and operations at a store level.

In the beginning, Eve was happy when lower-performing people left. The store profited, and operational indicators turned around as Ebony began working with those who stayed. Now that the store was producing well, Eve began changing. The "touch base" meetings with Ebony had become more and more critical of Ebony's direct and analytical style. Eve had switched from evaluating her on sales and profits to evaluating whether the store staff was happy, contented, staying on the job, and whether Ebony was getting along well with her coworkers. Eve looked at Ebony and wanted to see another amiable person.

Ebony's assessment profile revealed she was passionate and found personal value by helping others grow and achieve their professional potential. She felt successful when individuals on her team did well, and the team felt connected and displayed compassion, consideration, and kindness towards each other. She also had a strong motivator to measurable results and to be recognized for her contributions. Face-to-face communication was the key to engaging Ebony.

One of Ebony's significant complaints was that she hadn't received a raise in over three years. She was told by HR that she would get a salary increase in her first year, and when it came the time, they reneged. In a multitude of emails (rather than face-to-face conversations), she was told she was ineligible for an increase because she was at the top of the range, and there was nothing they could do. It was the straw that broke the camel's back. Ebony contacted me because she wanted to start interviewing for another job.

Ebony didn't recognize that her many years as the owner of a small business created a certain mindset as well as skill set. Her experiences gave her insights that others couldn't see nor understand. When senior management said, "Run the store like you own the business," in Ebony's mind, she really owned the business. She became personally invested in the success of her store and her team. She expected to get a bonus and salary increase for doing what hadn't been done before and sustaining measurable progress.

Entrepreneurs see a problem, own it completely, and work hard on fixing it as fast as possible, with a constant eye towards customer satisfaction and increasing efficiency. Ebony couldn't understand why other employees didn't see the same opportunities and the benefit of being part of a larger company. Ebony, who was once a high performing, highly engaged manager, was becoming increasingly frustrated and actively disengaged. From the discussions with Ebony, it was clear that Eve was also getting frustrated and didn't know what to do to assist and direct Ebony so she would once again be a top performer.

Eve could have broken the cycle by asking Ebony what changed for her. During the discussion, Eve could have helped Ebony see that her expectations were contributing to her frustration and dissatisfaction on the job. On the other hand, Eve should have known the broken promises were a contributing cause of Ebony's frustration. Based upon what Ebony shared with me, I was able to clearly define several additional issues:

- **Ebony was impatient** with people who couldn't see or take action on what she believed was "common sense."
- **Decisions were made at corporate office** by people who were working without understanding the impact on store operations. I helped Ebony understand that unless she changed her style of communicating with them, the lack of insight on their part only hurt her and her team.

- **Eve's criteria for good performance changed.** Maybe Eve should understand that high turnover was the cost of doing business, but she didn't. In the moment, Eve's opinion was that high turnover meant people didn't like their job. High turnover is the nature of retail, and if Ebony couldn't find a way to talk to Eve about that, then their relationship would continue to be strained.

- **Ebony was an excellent mentor.** A positive note, gleaned from the underlying factor driving turnover, was that Ebony had a reputation for developing excellent supervisors and managers. Many of her best people were recruited to other companies as assistant or store managers. Additionally, many of her best sales associates would go on to other careers because Ebony helped them clarify and hone their vision of success. This delighted Ebony as she understood retail sales jobs are steppingstones for many people.

- **Ebony needed stronger boundaries** and needed to enforce the rules across the board. Ebony was too understanding and collaborative with her team, thereby placing a strain on her management team's skills. The nature of retail is high turnover, and the rules are in place because a significant number of employees only want a job. They follow the rules, but if they are unclear, or a manager is lax with them, chaos ensues. Ebony's view, that everyone could be a high performer if you just allowed them to, didn't fit the facts.

**REMARKABLE LEADERSHIP EDGE:
COACHING CONVERSATION FOR MANAGERS**

The cultural values and virtues espoused by your company have to be a fit with the employees you hire. Your job is to ensure that how things get done day to day remains in line with the values stated in the vision and mission of your organization.

Managers... ask your team what they think their strengths are and then leverage that to make a difference in the organization. "How can you use your strength of xyz to bring better focus to your position, to the job at hand, within the values and virtues of our organization?"

Exercise:

As a manager, ask yourself these questions about each employee. Then ask them the same questions about themselves. The goal is to ensure you're both on the same page. The answers don't have to match, but they should be in the same ballpark.

- What is the organization's goal and your department's in particular?
- How do you measure your success?
- How do you measure productivity?
- What are the processes that cause you to work harder?
- What are your strengths?
- What do you do well but maybe dislike doing?
- What are your expectations of me, your team, and your performance?

Asking these questions is a good starting place. Be confident that once you've asked these questions, you'll figure out what it takes to manage each person/team more productively and create a more harmonious workplace.

MOVING ON...

One day Ebony revealed her new insights. "I was looking to others, thinking I wasn't good enough. Somehow, I thought my job defined me and should fulfill me. Just because I have a lot to offer doesn't mean I have to find one place to unload it all."

What Ebony realized was that she wanted to feel valued, listened to, and to work with people who cared about serving others as much as she did. The process of finding her passion led her to discover we all have many talents, motivations, and ways of seeing the world. For her, the old saying, "What works for one person may not work for another" became real.

Ebony is paid a good salary (helping her realize she is recognized as valuable in that she is paid at the top of the range), and has the reputation of bringing out the best in others so they can launch their careers. She also has the freedom to schedule and enjoy travel and be there for her aging parents. Ultimately, recognizing that combination was enough; she didn't have to be affirmed by her boss or the company. She accepted the value of her work/life integration.

Ebony had a newfound self-confidence and appreciation for the things her job did offer and the clarity to understand that no job defines us. Her strength ultimately comes from the culmination of life experience. The hard times, the good times, and even the longing for new and exciting things all taught her how to be a good manager and businesswoman. A job can only show the world one aspect of our abilities and provide a foundation for financial and lifestyle freedom. The rest is up to us.

PROFILE: WHAT WE GIVE UP TO BE ACCEPTED IN SEARCH OF THE PERFECT JOB

DENISEism:
Change is messy, but misery is optional.

I answered the call on the car's speaker phone. Dianne, a long-time client of mine, was in a panic. Dianne doesn't usually panic. Having worked her way to the top of the primarily male-dominated field of franchise real estate, this blonde-haired, blue-eyed Southerner is tough! When first meeting Dianne, men are drawn in by her Southern charm and engaging smile and soon find they are working with someone with a quick mind and determination, tough as nails with savvy negotiating skills.

At every milestone change in her career trajectory, Dianne persevered through the rough spots. Dianne learned that if someone can be guided toward mutually beneficial partnership agreements, the results are much more likely to be favorable.

Dianne won't stop working on the deal until everyone involved feels satisfied with the package. It doesn't matter if it's donuts or drugs, tacos or tires; Dianne puts together real estate packages that benefit everyone from the retailers/franchise owners to the landowners. This win, win, win approach, along with a track record of following through to make sure every detail is handled, has brought Dianne the hard-earned respect of her business peers. She is considered a top performer by her boss, franchise owners, and commercial real estate developers.

Two years prior, Dianne was in a role where, although the company was in turmoil nearly all the time, she really enjoyed the work. She had the freedom to control all aspects from vision to execution on the best projects. It was a well-liked brand with a very cool reputation. Everyone loved the product, and the growth potential was good.

She left the company when another round of layoffs was rumored. During this time of uncertainty, a recruiter reached out to her and offered her a role that felt very similar with a company that was more stable.

It turned out that accepting this offer was a disastrous mistake. Dianne found herself out of work by mutual agreement in six months.

Dianne rehired me to coach her through interviews, job negotiations, and for a few months after she began a new opportunity in the hospitality industry working for one of her former bosses, Sarah.

In the potential new role, Dianne would have thirty-five people in her organization doing the kind of work she once did. The role gave her the opportunity to be part of setting a new strategy for three companies, under the umbrella of a privately held woman-owned construction business.

Dianne thought the opportunity offered everything she wanted. She could now move from being a high performing individual, to an executive responsible for the company's direction. She wanted to have the full responsibility for managing a team reporting directly to her, instead of having members of her team report to two or three other executives. She thought it was great to be part of a fast-growing woman-owned and led company. Having been in the retail real estate industry all her life, Dianne recognized the challenges implicit in the new position, but it was clear the company hadn't kept up with the changes being made throughout the industry.

On this particular day in the car, Dianne's distress was about accepting the lucrative package from Sarah. "Do I go back to the someone who's 'crazy' I am familiar with, or do I keep looking for something new?" she asked me. Dianne was at a major fork in the career road.

I questioned, "Do you think you can do the work you want and need to do there?"

"I don't think Sarah is going to let go of the reins; she'll want to keep things the way she knows them now. I'm not sure I'll be able to bring in the technology that is needed to grow her business."

"Then you have your answer. It won't be good for you. It will be frustrating. You quit working for Sarah ten years ago because you couldn't implement the changes you felt were necessary. Right?"

Dianne thought a moment and hesitantly said, "Yeah. I know. But she says she's ready for me now and knows I can make a huge difference. She reached out to me! She's offering me a huge incentive package in addition to a nice base compensation salary. She said that she needs me to get them over this stagnation, to move to where the market is going to be. It could be a great opportunity." I could tell the challenge was intoxicating to Dianne.

I repeated more slowly, "Do you believe she will let you do what you think needs to be done?"

Dianne said, "She says she will. But if she doesn't, then the incentive package, which won't kick in for two years, won't yield anything."

"Is it worth taking the chance?" I asked.

"If she'll let me do what she needs to have done!" Dianne snapped. "This will be a big step up for me. It's a great challenge, and I can finally be on the leadership team."

This went back and forth for the rest of my drive home. I could sense Dianne's hesitation to making and sticking to a decision was all about security. A bird in the hand is worth more, etc. etc. but, I wondered, if that bird is a woodpecker that is constantly pecking at you… what then?

If Dianne was cognizant that working with Sarah was going to be challenging and the bonus structure was based on technology investments that may never come to pass, then the question becomes a risk vs. misery option. Do you take the risk on the potential to achieve all you want, while knowingly entering into a situation that may be fraught with misery from promises not kept? After a long discussion, Dianne told me she was going to pass on the role. *Good,* I thought. *That's what I hoped she'd do.*

A day later, I got a call from Dianne. The negotiations for the job were falling apart. Apparently, Dianne was still negotiating despite having told me she was passing. However, now, someone else (a man) had been hired at a higher salary and would be taking on a lot of what Dianne thought was to be included in her responsibilities. Dianne was confused and frustrated.

Since Dianne hadn't discontinued discussions, it seemed obvious that she was leaning towards the devil she already knew and the possibility of the dream opportunity and potential big payout. *Why was Dianne doing this to herself?* I wondered.

Dianne had been looking for a job for at least six months. Was the uncertainty of not knowing when she would be offered another job clouding her decision-making? Would that fear push her over to say yes to something that wasn't right for her? My role was not to make her decision but to help her through whatever she decided. I worked with her to at least improve the offer.

At the end of the third day, Dianne was proffered a job offer at a better salary, and the ability to implement the new technology was written into the agreement where quantifiable results were going to be used for the bonus payouts. She was told the hiring for the other position (the man) was put on hold. Dianne accepted the job.

"Desire can blind us to what's standing in front of us."

Fast forward….

Within two weeks, Dianne began to see that Sarah had not changed that much. Not only was an offer extended to hire the man, but now, Dianne would be reporting directly to him.

I advised Dianne that she could change her mind and quit. But Dianne was scared. Age discrimination is real, and Dianne was convincing herself that she was unmarketable. Too many of the interviews ended in "we like you and we'll let you know," only for her to read in the trade journals someone else was offered the position or never hearing what happened for months.

Plus, Dianne finally shared with me that she had been in a romantic relationship the first time around with Sarah, and this time things would be purely business. Dianne mistakenly thought their friendship and deeper connection would help them understand and trust each other this go-around.

Dianne kept her word and stayed on the job even after acknowledging it hadn't been the best decision.

Her first order of business was to meet with and assess the skills and career aspirations of those in her department, assess the real state of the business, and review the initiatives that had been started. Dianne and I talked about the financials and how costs were strangling the business. Dianne also needed to know what the new male boss was bringing to the table that clearly Sarah didn't see in her.

As the month progressed, Dianne realized that the business was in really bad shape. They were nowhere near ready to give the kind of service Sarah's own prime contractors demanded. The technology was insufficient and made it difficult to make decisions quickly or without an enormous expenditure of effort. Dianne's team was eager, but under skilled, as was her new boss.

A week after her new boss arrived, Dianne realized that she was being pushed to the side. She was not included in critical meetings, and he was meeting with key members of her team without her knowledge. She told me that the staff was claiming that they preferred having her as their boss.

Her new boss came from a high-profile consulting company and had little appetite for doing the detailed work required to take the company forward. "I advise and let others do," was his quip to Dianne as he laid out his plan for the company and Dianne's team.

A couple of weeks later, Dianne began to get really nervous. Her new boss was set on bringing in his own team, which would load the small company with too much overhead.

Additionally, his claim to having relationships within the industry turned out to be highly exaggerated. As Dianne explained it, "This is an industry of insiders, and everyone knows everyone else." Business relies on the strength of your reputation to get things done and help others get what they need done. Her new boss, she discovered, wasn't a known, credible entity in the industry.

Dianne was angry, hurt, scared, frustrated, and becoming more and more defensive every day. She talked about how she thought all the "isms"—gender, age, homophobia, even the fact that she was a Southerner—were playing against her.

She couldn't understand why she was being pigeon-holed and that her "friend," Sarah was listening to someone who didn't or couldn't have Sarah's best interest at heart. The final straw came when Sarah fired one of Dianne's direct reports without telling Dianne first. She learned accidentally when the HR Director asked her about a replacement the next day.

Dianne called me, furious. "I'm done! This is total BS! Sarah is not changing and in fact, I think she is only getting worse."

"What do you want to do?" I asked.

"I'm quitting! This place is imploding, and it will not take me down with it."

"Okay. To keep your integrity intact, you have to talk openly with Sarah. Never let it be said that your boss or the company didn't know your opinion. They may not like your opinion but never surprise them. If you do, trust is broken, and that is something that is hard to repair."

"Yeah... yeah... yeah. Neither of them feels that way about me. They don't mind doing things without consideration of me, my expertise, or my people. This is just crap!" Dianne spewed.

"Be that as it may, you have to stay true to yourself, and just quitting without sharing your concerns with Sarah is not you. At some point in the future, it would eat at you. This is a small industry and if you two have unresolved issues between you, it will look like a "girl fight" to others as they won't know why you two are angry at each other."

Dianne packed up her belongings and put them in her car. Later that evening she stopped in to see Sarah. They had a long talk, which ended with Dianne telling Sarah she really did have her best interest at heart, but she wasn't so sure about others she'd hired. Dianne went over parts of her strategic plan and talked openly about their working relationship. They talked about what went right and how it got "off track." On the ride home, Dianne called me to say she thought it went well, given the circumstances.

In the meantime, Dianne and I worked to find the next, right opportunity for her. Six months later Dianne accepted a role with a company outside of the industry. She is thriving there.

REMARKABLE LEADERSHIP LESSONS

- **Keep skills relevant and growing.** Dianne decided that if she was going to remain marketable, she had to find a role that would allow her to develop and demonstrate her leadership and operational skills.

- **Nothing is forever.** She accepted that no decision is forever and when new information presents itself, there is nothing wrong with changing your mind.
- **Get over it! Keep moving forward.** Dianne learned that her experiences and the regret she had over leaving a great company was actually holding her back from getting another job.
- **If you don't ask, you don't get.** Dianne also learned that you have to be clear on what you want and ask for it. Today, she still struggles with how to ask, but she definitely is over not knowing what to ask for.
- **Trust your gut.** Dianne was delaying making a decision about the job with Sarah because her instincts were telling her it wasn't a good fit. Past experience told her it wasn't a good fit. Her brain wanted to believe the words she was hearing. Her logical mind was seduced by the challenges being promised. But her instincts saw what her logical mind wouldn't.

THE POWER OF NONVERBAL COMMUNICATION

DENISEism:
You matter!

Everything we learn is a result of experiences from our childhood. Between ages two to eleven, we are like sponges. We soak up all kinds of experiences, and yet our ability to process the information—sense making—comes later in life when we are on our own, attempting to recreate what we think we learned. The foundation for how we make sense of the world (such as connections and decisions) is a combination of what we experienced during that time.

My Nana (maternal grandmother) and Aunt Karen always told me to make sure I was a good person, to be kind, and to speak clearly. Their words meant a lot to me.

James Brown sang, "Say it loud; I'm black and I'm proud!" At the same time, my friends teased me, "Not so bright; you know you ain't right."

I didn't see myself as a pretty girl. Here I was with big eyes, big forehead, big clumsy feet, dark-skinned, in a world where light-skinned was considered beautiful. I was often reminded of my faults by my friends when they wanted to hurt me. They would say, "You're a black thang" or hold up a brown paper bag and say, "You don't pass."

My hair was (and is) kinky, and for the most part, it was the most redeeming thing I had going on, as it was longer than most.

Nana shopped at Marshall Fields. I remember being at her home on 47th and St. Lawrence when she would send out bits of wisdom while we worked in the kitchen, sat around her apartment, while eating or taking walks together: "Wear the best you can." "Don't buy your clothes for today but for every day." "You'll look classy with timeless pieces." She always said, "When you go into the store, act like you can afford to buy what you want. Never ask 'how much does it cost?' Because if you have to ask... then you can't afford it."

Nana's words passed through my mind as I sat in our Rambler station wagon next to my daddy as we drove through the streets of Chicago on our way to my first formal interview. I really wanted to be classy and impressive, but how was I to follow Nana's advice when I was dressed in a Girl Scout uniform? My mother told me the world would judge me based upon how I looked. That did not instill confidence in me! In that moment, I doubted that she really loved me. How little I knew that my mother's words were so true, and in a matter of days, life would prove her right.

I was thirteen and my father and I were headed to *that* side of town. Racism and segregation were alive and well in Chicago, despite civil rights progress. The "colored only" signs may not have been visible any longer, but the expectation remained. As a person of color, there were sides of town you didn't go to after dark without the real threat of harm. There were jobs for which you were qualified, and other jobs (no matter how skilled on paper you may have been) for which you were never quite qualified enough.

Here I was on my way to be interviewed. You see, I was in the running to be selected as Chicago's south side representative for the Girl Scouts. My troop leader nominated me, and although at the time I didn't really understand what that meant, I could tell from the way my mother and father reacted, it was a big deal.

For more than two weeks, my mother spent her time "training me" to be a polished young lady. After school I would come home and she would put a book on my head and have me walk with my shoulders back, chin up, stomach pulled in, and she kept shouting at me to "pick up your feet," as I attempted to glide from the living room to the kitchen and back again.

I had to walk, talk, and balance that book on my head as I did part of my chores. Then I was to turn and strike a pose of confidence. As commanded, I'd turn but then the book would fall off my head and I'd strike some kind of pose as I caught the book. Did that look like confidence? I don't think so. I was reprimanded, "Do it again, and this time don't drop the book!"

How would I know what looked like a "confident pose" when I couldn't see myself? We didn't have a floor length mirror! At best I could see my reflection out of the corner of my eye as I passed the glass hutch in the dining room. As I look back on it all, I remember being aware that this was odd.

There were no questions to practice answering for the Girl Scout interview. My parents' advice was that I was just meant to be model perfect. I think neither of my parents knew about interviewing or how to help me pass this test.

About three days before the interview, I was still trying to keep that Encyclopedia Britannica on my head. I remember it falling off and my mother (who had this look that could stop an elephant in its tracks), whipped her head around and stiffened her back, her mouth and jaw tightened. But it was her eyes that made my blood run cold and fear shimmy up my back.

As I reached down to get the "stupid book," I must have huffed one time too many. My mother did not disappoint in sharing her disapproval. "Denise Jeanna Williams! Getting angry at the book doesn't help you one bit! Girl," she continued, "there will be no place in this lifetime that you will not be judged by how you look and carry yourself. Pick up that book… put it on your head, and keep it balanced, or else!"

I looked at her and all I could think was *She's so old-fashioned.* Dr. Martin Luther King had just told us to judge people by the content of their character not by the color of their skin. How could my mother be so backwards as to not notice that the world was changing?

As my father continued the drive north on 95th Street to what was then a community center, I sat erect and tense. We were headed to a place where I wasn't sure if it was safe for us, but my dad didn't seem too nervous, so I took comfort that most likely it would be fine. However, I had something else to worry about and it consumed every fiber of my being.

The day before the interview, I had gone to the closet to get my Girl Scout beret. When I reached up to pull down the hat from behind a bunch of quilts, a sharp pain shot up my back and gripped my neck in a viselike hold. I'd never felt anything like it (and to my delight haven't felt anything like it since). I stood perfectly still in front of that closet, because to move meant the pain would pierce me like a knife and move up to my brain.

For an instant, I thought about calling out for help, but after a bit of consideration, didn't. I was the only girl of African American descent who was selected to be interviewed for the high honor of representing our area at a national event. There was no way I could back out; there was only going forward. So, I stood there totally pained, with tears coming down my face and a silent cry caught in my throat as I slowly moved to pick up the quilts and my beret.

I prayed for relief. "Dear God, please oh please, don't let me have to tell my mother about this. Please take this pain away and make it so I can interview tomorrow. I promise whatever you want, I'll do it."

That night I didn't get much sleep. Being up early, I met dad at the kitchen table. He'd just put up the coffee, and I could hear the pluck, pluck, pluck from the coffee pot. As usual he took a cup into my mother as she completed her morning rituals in the bedroom and bathroom.

My face must have been tear-streaked because he looked up and said, "There's nothing to worry about. Just do your best and it will be good enough."

I gave him a stiff smile. I moved toward the car without ever moving my neck, back, nor raising my arms as to do so meant sheer hellish pain that would run right through me.

Sitting in the front seat as the car headed toward the assigned destination, I wondered just how I was going to carry out this nearly impossible feat. I was sure they would discover I was in pain and most certainly disqualify me.

My father pulled in front of the community center, and I disembarked slowly. I walked to the door and looked back at him, but he'd already pulled off, as being on Kedzie Avenue wasn't necessarily safe for people like us. Stories of black people being beaten up or arrested for being on the wrong side of town were still common on the news.

As a safety precaution, my father said he'd be in the nearby park and not wait on the street. "When you finish, just come out and stand on the stairs and I'll see you. As soon as possible, I'll get to you and then it will be all over. You can get back home and take that uniform off. Don't be nervous, baby. Remember, however it turns out, it just does. You'll be fine and so will I." I needed that wisdom and reassurance!

I had to pull hard to open the huge cumbersome doors, wincing in pain. As I stepped into the hallway, I saw a couple of other Girl Scouts in the standard green uniform, but mostly many white adult females. Some were dressed in Scout leader's uniforms and some in dresses.

I'm positive I looked out of place. Here was this little black girl in a Girl Scout uniform walking towards them like she had a stick up her butt. My back erect, head high, and eyes forward not because I was confident, but because if I didn't stand that way, many bolts of pain would shoot up my back.

I walked up to a woman in a Scout leader's uniform and told her I was there for the interviews. She asked me for my name and then told me to have a seat. As I looked around, I realized sitting wasn't in the cards. The chairs were too hard, and I didn't know if I could stand up again once I sat. I just mumbled, "I'll stand over there and wait."

After what felt like forever, my name was called. I walked into the interview room and faced three stern-looking women sitting behind a long rectangular table. Papers where they had been writing notes about the last girl, and the girls before that, were splayed out in front of them.

It was my turn. I stood perfectly still, praying I could answer without crying out; I needed to focus. I wish I could say I remembered the questions, that my answers were inspiring, but I don't remember anything specific at all. What I do remember is the essence of the meeting.

There were questions. I gave answers. I looked each person in the eye, turning full body towards them because I couldn't turn my head. I remember walking back and forth as my mother had instructed. And then it was over.

The first woman—the one who greeted me in the hall—said thank you. I remember walking out wondering how was I going to tell my mother I failed? The interviewers weren't friendly. They didn't even seem to pay attention to me. No smiles. No warmth. A nod here and there and LOTS of writing.

All I felt was the weight of judgment and a really strong desire to just get out of there, so I could figure out what to do about my back pain.

I walked stiffly to the door, opened it, and walked through to the next door, which led out of the building. I was hoping my dad was nearby and I could just get in the car and go home.

Within minutes, I saw the familiar Rambler turn the corner and pull up to the curb. I reached for the door handle and when I went to pull the door open, I went blind with the pain. This time my dad must have seen my face because I saw him run around the front of the car to get me. I couldn't hold back the waterworks any longer. He grabbed me yelling, "What's wrong? What's wrong? Why are you crying?"

I confessed to the pain and my father, my protector, stood there for a minute, processing. Once he recognized that nothing horrible had happened in the building, he wrapped my arms around his shoulders and his around me, lifted me up, and squeezed till I snapped! And then the pain was gone. I was freed. RELIEF!

He explained that I just had a crick in my back, as if it was nothing at all. Then he asked, as he opened the car door for me to get in, how I did with the interview. The important stuff!

The drive home was the best I ever remembered. I told him I really didn't know how it went. And then I told him about the room and the women and the lack of any clues to understand whether I did well or poorly.

A few days later, I learned that I had been selected to be a member of the team of girls heading to California to represent Chicago, Illinois—the first African American girl from Chicago to join this team.

My mom later found out that what the judges remembered about me was my poise and posture. "Out of all the girls, you had the best posture and you were so poised," she said. While mom was satisfied that her encyclopedia training helped me pass the test, only my dad and I knew the real reason for my posture and poised presentation.

What I learned from the whole experience was that your physical presence and mannerisms matter as much as what you say. The ability to communicate is more than just words.

Every day I have to choose to step up and show out. It doesn't matter how unqualified I may feel or how much pain I may be in. My whole self makes an impression. My physical being, words, tone, facial expressions… every bit of me sends a message to others, telling them who I am and what matters to me. The essence of connecting and communicating with others is rooted in our ability to accept who we are and have the courage to put ourselves out there, knowing there's a possibility we will not be selected—or liked.

NONVERBAL COMMUNICATION

Many years after my Girl Scout triumph, I attended a communications class. The instructor pointed to the screen and said that our nonverbal clues were far more important than what we said. I listened intently. Research from professor Albert Mehrabian (in the 1960s) stated that:

- 55 percent of how people communicate is based upon body language
- 38 percent is based on tone
- 7 percent is based upon the words we speak.

I've since heard this data many times, and if you've taken a communications class, then you've also heard these same statistics. Well it turns out, it is another statistic that is often quoted, but is not *quite* right.

Mehrabian completed a series of small research studies, trying to figure out the impact of verbal communication on credibility. Later, in 1971, he wrote a book called *Silent Messages*, where he used his research to try to convey that when your body language and tone are inconsistent with your words, you wind up with a credibility problem. Your audience (whether one person or thousands) will doubt what you say.

Since the Mehrabian book was published, other social scientists have doubted that our presence is 12.5 times more powerful than our words, and have conducted more complex and extensive studies, only to find out that indeed, what you say is less important than how you say it. When put that way, it makes sense.

Whenever we meet someone, our body automatically goes into sensing mode. In less than .007 seconds, we sense the energy around us. Have you ever walked into a room where a couple of people have been talking and they immediately stop as you enter hearing range? Go back to that moment in your mind. Could you determine whether they were in an argument or having a friendly secret chat that you interrupted? What were you thinking would be the answer when you probably asked, "Hey, what are you doing?"

By seven seconds, our brain has run through our past experiences, married them with our beliefs, values, and expectations, and we instantly know whether we're welcome or not.

What the Girl Scout interview panel reacted to was the combination of visual clues that conveyed and matched their belief of what a confident and poised person looks and feels like.

Social psychologists Dana Carney and Judith Hall have carefully studied powerful and powerless body language. If you're in the Human Resources profession, you're likely to hear "I know it when I see it," as the answer a manager will give when you ask them to describe the kind of person who's ready for a promotion or greater responsibility.

We have an expectation that high-powered, highly confident people initiate handshakes, make more and longer eye contact, have erect and open posture, lean forward, and orient the body and head toward others.

Amy Cuddy, a Harvard Business School professor and social psychologist, studies how nonverbal behavior and snap judgments influence people. In her book *Presence: Bringing your Boldest Self to Your Biggest Challenges*, she writes about power poses. These positions are "so strong they neutralize or overcome other signs of a person's status." For example, when we slump and look away, it conveys a lower status, a lack of confidence, and less power. These power positions seem to be universal.

Jessica Tracy a professor of psychology at the University of British Columbia, and her colleagues study pride. They've found "pride takes over the whole body." The expanded and upright posture, head tilted slightly upward, and a small smile have been shown to universally be a signal of pride, confidence, and trustworthiness.

All this is not to say that my mother was totally right about being judged by how you present yourself, and that I misunderstood the words of Dr. Martin Luther King, Jr, who said we are judged by the content of our character. What Dr. King knew, was that earning trust is a process. Trust is determined by your actions over time. To be judged by the content of our character requires us to pay attention to and be mindful of our actions.

Those evaluators at the table with the glowering faces didn't know me. They knew me only by my reputation… what my Scout leader told them. They witnessed my stiff, erect posture, my head held high and tilted slightly upward as if I had a book resting on my skull. The combination of my body position along with a good reputation signaled that I was confident, poised, and capable of doing the job. Decision made.

In day-to-day business interactions, just like the Girl Scout judges, people will evaluate you based on the reputation that precedes you, along with how you present yourself. The words you deliver will either confirm the decision they had in mind before you arrived or will cause them to change their minds. Whether preparing to pitch to a new client, present a report to coworkers, your supervisors, the board, or conduct a family meeting, remember that it's the combination of all the factors that will impact the evaluator/listener's final decision.

REMARKABLE LEADERSHIP LESSON

How We Determine Trust

- Your character determines your actions
- Your actions determine your reputation
- Your reputation is nonverbal communication signaling who you are and what to expect, because we cannot read your mind

---

SECTION II
MINDSET, BACKGROUND, CULTURE GOING FROM ME TO WE

IDEAS  ACTION

FEAR IS A HEAVY COAT WE WEAR

DENISEism:
Unmasking the many faces of fear: Desire, self-confidence, jokes, silence, compliance, and anger

---

Early in my career my first response was to defend and attack. Over time, I learned to use words as my weapon, but I also learned from Ms. Louise (aka Mom) that looks could kill. In hindsight I can say I was probably pretty good at sensing and defending against attacks. Being a 5'1", 103-pound black woman, working in all-male industries like the building and construction trades for the union, in a non-union state in the South, taught me that most situations could go bad pretty quickly. I had to learn to "fight" in business mode, not with my fists. I've had to face down men who both overtly and subtly threatened me, aiming to test my resolve.

CRANE CONFLICT

One day while working on a job site, I was in a crane basket suspended high over the ground with a 6' tall white man who had just threatened me by saying something like… how easy it would be for me to suddenly slip and fall over the side. You see, my job was to increase the number of women and minorities working on federally funded sites. Since I represented the building and construction trade council in Arkansas (in the 1980s) you can imagine there were a few people who didn't think I had a right to promote these changes, nor did they like the idea of accepting people who didn't look like them.

As I felt this man's contempt from across the bucket and heard threatening words slowly and deliberately emerge from his lips as we lifted into the air, I could feel fear well up in me. My response was to move into "street" mode. I gave him a steely-eyed glare, set a black woman's stance that signaled "I'm ready," and barked a resolved and slowly enunciated statement: "If I go, you bet you'll go with me, and yo mama is gonna mourn her baby boy." I looked from his eyes, down his body to his feet, in a visual exclamation point. Period. End of statement. When my eyes came back up to his, I'm not sure if I scared him or not, but I can say it made him lift his icy gaze, laugh, and lower the crane so I could get off. I did not let myself shake or wobble as I stomped (as much as a tiny woman can emphatically stomp) off until I could find a place to reset my meter and get back to stable!

LIGHTS OUT

Another time, I was working for AFLCIO, in the building trades, and as I was leaving the job site, I saw people practicing shooting with guns. Real guns. I honestly didn't think much of it. I remember hearing clicks/beeps as I backed out of my parking spot and then drove out of the lot.

A couple of weeks later, I asked my brother to fix my rear car light for me. After a quick inspection, he said "Denise, your lights have been blown out with a gun! Where were you?"

I said, "What are you talking about? Are you joking with me?"

He opened his palm and showed me. "Here are the bullets."

As I was driving away from that construction site, those men were shooting at my car, laughing, like I was a training target! Were they racist? Were they sexist? Misogynistic? Were they testing my courage to stand up to them because we were in a macho world of hard hats and danger?

That history is what I bring to work every day and in every new situation. My first thoughts when I meet someone who isn't like me are: Are you an ally? Or are you a racist? Or waiting for an excuse to challenge me? Or do you think these behaviors are funny? Are you a sexist? Do you think I'm here as a plaything for you to toy with? Do you respect me as an equal? Are you going to try to intimidate me into a submissive role because you think all women should be submissive and are less-than? Am I going to have to work three times as hard as anyone else here because I'm a woman and get paid less for it anyway?

Ultimately, I need to know if you are okay with these behaviors that make me feel any of these things, whether dished out by you or anyone on your team or in the organization.

This is what I need to process in my head as I'm having my conversations with new people in my life, and what my clients have to process as they work each day with coworkers, supervisors, clients/customers.

Faster than a blink of the eye, with each interaction, I have to determine if I will stay and fight, or will I flee? The flight response is just what you think… to literally run away. Your body actually moves your blood supply to your limbs so that you can flee. At work, you might leave the room. You might stop talking and your mind becomes preoccupied with thoughts only about how you will get away from the threatening personality in front of you.

It's a conversation that many African Americans frequently have with themselves and others. Safety—physical and mental—is a concern uppermost in our minds. This is also true for many women. In a country that has yet to realize the importance of having healing conversations, the lines defining inappropriate behavior (sexual abuse, harassment) are blurry. Blurry lines make all of us, especially white men, uncomfortable.

We live in a country that has yet to address its past abuses and present-day statutory laws that keep some marginalized and give others an advantage based on the color of their skin or biological gender. Turning a blind (color or gender) eye only adds more hurt on top of injury. We come to work, attend events, and travel in our cars wondering when (not if), and how to handle ourselves when faced with the small and big assaults on our humanity. The result often leads us to mute our full potential. As an employer, a leader, we get the best from our people by creating a safe space at work.

REMARKABLE LEADERSHIP EDGE: ENGAGING EMPLOYEE FEEDBACK

Remarkable leaders constantly engage their employees in cocreating a workspace that feels safe and has clearly defined conversational tactics, ground rules, and definitions.

- Pull together department managers to discuss their thoughts on what is needed to create an equitable culture. An equitable culture answers the question: How do we ensure we are recognizing individual contributions while acknowledging that it takes a team of people working together, to manifest a common vision?
- Bring in an outside facilitator to teach your team how to listen and really hear the unedited, uncensored feedback of the team members to clarify the potential hurdles that need to be overcome.
- Review literature and multimedia materials focused on what other organizations have done (both within your industry and in the more varied general business world), to understand the range of options available.
- Behaviors and cultures have consequences (both upside and downside). Create a safe space on an ongoing basis, for employees to air their areas of concern and tell the stories of how work gets done, and who gets recognized and rewarded for specific behaviors and results.

CULTURE EATS STRATEGY EVERY TIME

DENISEism:
Perspective, perspective... (did I mention
perspective?) drives expectations.

Have you ever just agreed with or done something that you didn't believe in just to get the other person to stop talking, or because you believe it was the best way to avoid retaliation or consequences down the line?

Have you ever just done something to get it over with because you felt the consequences of *not* doing it were dire? This is commonly seen with people in abusive relationships. You've probably heard stories of women who had sex with their lover right after a physical fight. Police and domestic abuse counselors report that victims of domestic violence will often blame themselves as the reason for their abuser's behaviors.

HOW WE DO THINGS AROUND HERE

A former client, May, a Chinese American woman in her mid-forties, began a new position as part of a team and quickly became the high performer. She came to me when a colleague quietly and gently let her know that, "Working that hard is not what we do around here."

May was later approached by a "friendly" team member who said the team didn't like the new supervisor, which seemed to translate into, "WE are all in agreement on this, you understand?" It's the old, play-along-to-get-along routine. Apparently, there were some questions about the supervisor's management style. When May said she thought he was a good supervisor, her coworker began pointing out all the bad decisions the supervisor had made and how he was not giving them the resources to do the work, always wanting more and more. My client got the distinct feeling that she was being coached to see his management style as a problem.

The next week HR got wind of the supervisor's unfair and "bad management style." As an investigation ensued, May heard her coworkers say they were going to get rid of him.

The HR department conducted a complete investigation, asking questions about the supervisor's performance to all the people on the team. May's coworkers told HR that the supervisor was angry in meetings, picking favorites, and insisting that the team work faster and harder.

May observed that her coworkers were being lazy and missing deadlines. They would commit to completing assignments and then not do them. She saw the boss be stern and reprimand the pertinent employees after missing deadlines four or five times. Her boss, being pushed by his own supervisor, needed the team to get the work done. Instead the team ganged up to get him out instead of them having to be accountable for their work.

Trust between the supervisor and subordinate group impacts the performance review and work process. Completion of projects and hitting deadlines impacts results and productivity. It could be that if the supervisor was coached better, he could have gotten the instigator out and survived the investigation.

During our next coaching session, May struggled. She did share with the investigators that she thought the manager was doing a good job, while being careful not to praise him too much. But she didn't share what her coworkers had said to her, how they were trying to influence her, about the culture of the work team. May told her truth but questioned whether she told THE truth.

May could not trust her coworkers, nor could she trust that the company would be fair and protect her if she didn't do as the informal leaders on the team wanted. May loved her work and felt that doing less than your best was irresponsible. Although there was a compliance hotline for employees to use to report unusual or questionable activities, May (and others) didn't call the line because they didn't feel like they could report anything without retaliation.

From the outside, the group appeared to function well. May talked about all the effort senior management spent telling employees they were valued, talking about the values of teamwork, collaboration, respect, and high performance being rewarded. Listening to this, "we went to a seminar and this is what we're supposed to believe" vision sounded good but coping with the reality that it was only just talk, was sickening her.

"How could they not know?" she asked me. How could senior management and HR not know what was going on right in front of them?

May didn't understand why her supervisor asking for deadlines was a bad thing. May ultimately quit the job because of the bad taste in her mouth. She left after the workgroup succeeded in getting the supervisor demoted and he was moved to another work group. May worried that her coworkers would do the same thing to her if she ever fell out of favor with them. Eventually her former supervisor quit also.

REMARKABLE LEADERSHIP LESSONS

May's employer spent a lot of time and money to recruit and train May only to lose her along with a good supervisor, (and probably others) because of disengaged employees. May's departure should be classified as a regrettable turnover. Regrettable turnover is a classification that lets management see how many and where they are losing top talent. Understanding why people like May leave, provides some insights into how to improve employee engagement.

- **Consider the behavior of the coworkers.** As you read the story, you may have felt compassion for the male supervisor and contempt for the behavior of May's coworkers. The one thing we will never know is their intentions or motives: Were the subordinates lazy and mean-spirited? Did the supervisor hold them to an unfair standard? Since we can't read minds (and we should stop acting like we can), we have to ask good questions and have an open mind to the possibility that what we think is happening doesn't tell us why it is happening nor how to change results.

- **Understanding and being able to identify actively disengaged employees is critical.** According to Gallup, employees who are actively disengaged make up about 12-15 percent of your workforce. They are also the most difficult to get rid of because very few executives have a clear idea of what constitutes disengagement or its impact on productivity, costs, quality, and performance. Actively disengaged employees are not poor performers. To the contrary. They generally are satisfactorily doing their work. The only way to identify them is to become skilled at seeing, talking about, and dealing with their behavior in the workplace.

ROLE MODELS SET OUR EXPECTATIONS CONSCIOUSLY AND UNCONSCIOUSLY

DENISEism:
We define leaders by the role models we cherish.

Women tend to be rewarded for leadership behaviors like compassion, not using harsh language, being sensitive to the needs of others, loyalty, warmth, understanding, and tenderness. Men, on the other hand, are rewarded for directness, overconfidence, competitiveness, analytics, forcefulness, and defending their position.

Once I was asked by a female store manager to facilitate a leadership workshop for her store supervisors. Of the people who attended the workshop, only one supervisor was a man. The participants ranged in age from twenty-one to fifty-one.

I asked them, who was the best leader they knew? The women in their twenties responded: "My mother." I noticed, other than a teacher, these women didn't have any role models. The women over thirty-five and the man named a variety of people from all walks of life.

Participants were then asked to describe leadership behaviors that, in their opinion, worked. The women under thirty-five talked about the above listed behaviors, while the women over thirty-five talked about achieving results, directness, and clearly communicating a point of view.

We then talked about how to define what a leader does. The exercise enabled them to recognize how their own perspective on what good leadership looks like, impacted how they led and was the basis for their performance expectations and that of their leaders. We continued with a healthy discussion on how to measure the job performance and developed a shared understanding around leadership behaviors, along with how our differing perspectives impacted the operations. Afterwards, we developed a shared meaning of what leadership behaviors were needed, given the people they supervised and the expectations on performance by corporate.

The end result was a dramatic reduction in conflict, tension, and miscommunication amongst the management team and employees. The woman who brought me in said the team now had a common language and set expectations on their roles as leaders. They were more supportive of each other, often using the code words developed during the session to remind each other about their "agreed upon behaviors and standards of conduct."

WHAT DOES IT TAKE
TO CHANGE YOUR MIND?

The separation of the mind and body is one of the reasons humans have such a difficult time working together. On the one hand, our subconscious mind or "gut," reacts before we're conscious about the reaction. We rationalize what we are feeling with stories based upon our past experience and knowledge.

When your gut says you're in a dangerous situation—"I shouldn't trust you"—but your brain explains it away—"Oh no I must be wrong; you're a good person," what do you do? When that feeling in your gut tells you something is off, but your brain makes light of it, do you dismiss what you're feeling because there's nothing tangible there, or do you pause (even stop), and reflect on what you're feeling? Because the words sound like there's no harm intended, yet I'm feeling daggers all over my body. Will you dismiss your gut because the words are what you would expect to hear, only to later kick yourself when you realize your gut instinct was right?

As a child you're taught that what you see is not important. Kids blurt out what they see: "You're fat. She's ugly. He stinks." First thing our parents or other adults in our lives say? "Don't say that. That's impolite. That person is [insert your own explanation]." It's these lessons that teach us to suppress the truth, and to be careful of what we say. In our effort to live in a "polite society" we choose to remain silent rather than speaking the truth for fear of hurting someone and them hurting us. We trust those like us, faster than those who are different.

I've learned that the most valuable skill you can acquire is the ability to know when it's time to change your mind and then do it. When blind spots emerge or you find out what you believed for years isn't true any longer, what do you do?

MY TRUTH SHARING

At one point, briefly, I was homeless. Everybody that knows me can't believe it. "Why were you homeless?" Well, I accepted an assignment for a job in the Cincinnati area. The company paid for relocation, but I had to find an apartment to live in. I did what most people do and that was look at the open listings. I'd called ahead and made arrangements to see an apartment that met my budget and criteria and scheduled to meet the landlord.

On the phone setting up the appointment, the people were all cheery and welcoming. But as soon as they saw me, suddenly the apartment was already rented... they said.

For two and half weeks I had to live in my car, going from building to building, and after finding apartments available on the phone, I showed up to find they had already been rented. And yet I went to work every day like nothing was wrong.

When my boss, Ron, found out, he went ballistic. First, he wanted to know why I, his newly hired executive, didn't tell him. But my life experience taught me you don't share that kind of stuff. I was taught we leave our personal life at the door. It was what I was told, and sadly I've told others the same thing.

It turned out that Ron, a white man who had a reputation as an up-and-coming executive, was really caring. Although he didn't help me find a home, from that moment on, he adopted a policy of making sure I felt welcomed wherever I went. This included terminating the company membership at a country club when he discovered I wasn't allowed to be there because I was a woman.

"THEY" ARE TURNING ON "US"

I have experienced the world through the eyes of a minority, as a person of color, and a woman, along with being short, and still had moments where I was oblivious to other people's issues. I met Pete when I worked at Monsanto. Pete is 5'10, white, nice-looking, a distinguished scientist.

Something happened in the news, maybe Al Sharpton said something, and Pete marched into my HR office and began ranting about how terrible "they" *all* are when you're a minority. "They're turning on us!"

As I'm listening to this white man getting worked up about our oppressive society, I'm confused and wondering, "What? Is he Jewish? What minority is he? What are you talking about, dude?" I literally had no clue. Pete left, having expelled all his anger into the air around me, and I turned to my secretary and said, "He was going on about how they're turning on 'us;' things ain't going right for us as minorities. Is he Jewish?" I asked her.

She looked at me, exasperated, and said, "He's gay, Denise!" I felt flummoxed. He was gay and I had no idea. I knew he was married. It never dawned on me that he was married to a man!

Whatever baggage and fears Pete had in his day-to-day life, at work he kept them hidden. Could his worry have impacted his performance? Maybe. But it hadn't to the degree that anyone complained or noticed.

Sometimes an individual's fears, anxieties, and home life overflow into work productivity.

Well-meaning HR people have implemented diversity awareness programs in an attempt to get through some of this clutter in our heads. But I don't like most of these programs. All these stories get told from the heart, bared to everyone, everybody is crying. White people are crying "I'm so sorry! I didn't know!"

Okay, great. And for about a week, they work on being more aware of what they're saying or how they react, but then they go back to who they were because no behavior has been changed. It was a workshop, a weekend, a retreat. But then the guilt shows up. So now what used to be a tolerable relationship has now become hugely defensive on all levels. I bared my soul, you promised to change, now you haven't changed, you're mad at me for making you feel bad, and now you're doing it again. Betrayal.

REMARKABLE LEADERSHIP LESSONS

Examine your blind spots. These experiences are part of *my* story. What's your story? Each of us has a story. When you think about all the stories that are being carted around in an office, it's really a miracle that anything actually ever gets done!

All of these dynamics are what people are bringing in to work with them and unfortunately, from an HR point of view, there is no way that HR can manage every situation. In designing a workplace culture, ensure there is a way for people to be humans, have lives outside work, and still be held accountable for performance. Some suggestions:

- **Gather and review data**, business results, and stories that provide insights on what is considered acceptable and unacceptable behavior. Use the collected stories to see how your people policies, decision-making, productive conflict and disagreement reflect your company values, mission statements, and ability to do business.
- **With a critical eye, examine how are decisions made?** Top down, experts, or are those in authority allowed to make

exceptions? Is it clear at every meeting what is expected, what decisions are made, and who is to carry out the decisions? Is the information provided in a balanced way, or do executives regularly hear positive spins on what's happening?

- **What are acceptable excuses for missing expectations?** Are managers allowed to say they can't find good people, talented women and minorities, and yet it is frowned upon if they say they can't solve a product or service defect problem?

- **Individual vs. group recognition:** Do the decisions you make about people policies, processes such as recruiting and performance management, reward individual success at the expense of collaboration, communication and support?

- **Next step after collecting data:** If you use personality assessments such as the DiSC, what are the expectations for using the information gleaned? Are your teams made up of diverse thinkers and people who have different backgrounds? Is it expected that people know how to individually and collectively work through ideas or problems and acknowledge success? Are the results viewed through a culturally sensitive and enlightened lens?

As human beings we may prefer to be with people who are just like us. We sort everyone into a category that allows us to quickly determine how we will deal with them. It's natural. We are also addicted to being right. These two behavioral drivers often cause us to surround ourselves with people who look like us, have experiences similar to us, and make us comfortable. However, thought leadership comes from moving out of our comfort zones to seeking different experiences and applying them in unexpected ways. When's the last time you let go of a preconceived idea? Who are the people you want to be like, and who whispers in your subconscious ear, telling you what to aspire to be, do, and say? Is it time for you to change your mind?

SECTION III
INFLUENCING AND CHANGING OTHERS

IDEAS  ACTION

PROFILE: WHAT YOU DO IS MORE IMPORTANT THAN WHAT YOU SAY

DENISEism:
We make decisions on how to treat others
based upon our values. Others judge us
based on the impact of our behavior.

I was delighted to hear from a former client, Marcia. I'd worked with Marcia a few years earlier when she was concerned about her career in Human Resources. That experience ultimately became the turning point in Marcia's career. When Marcia said that she was working with the Fortune 100 financial services giant and needed my coaching services for a high-performance, high potential employee [HIPO], Velinda, I realized our reconnection wasn't just a catch-up session. I stopped working and sat down with a cup of coffee to listen.

Marcia shared that Velinda had been an all-star for more than twenty years and had suddenly, with the arrival of a new supervisor, started getting less than stellar reviews and the performance statistics reflected a negative change. Would I please go meet with her and see if I could help?

After passing through layer upon layer of security, I met Velinda in a beautiful, airy atrium. Velinda, only 5'2" tall and thin-boned carried herself like the stately atrium trees, straight and graceful. Like the polished floors and perfectly groomed florals, Velinda wore a colorful but conservative sweater set with slacks and heels. Simple makeup accentuated her natural vibrancy and youthful appearance, though she was nearing retirement at sixty-five in just a few more years. Velinda's spiky short dark hair was cut in a way that reminded me of Jennifer Hudson, whom I've always admired for her sense of style.

Velinda greeted me with an easy smile and offered a tour of the campus. As we walked through the gardens, I peeked in the offices to see top-of-the-line employee amenities, stylish office furniture and décor. Velinda greeted people everywhere. She praised her company. She talked about finding the perfect job at a company she loved, that worked to ensure she was happy. She had only a few years before retiring and had no ambitions of taking on a larger role at the company. Velinda was happy doing what she did so well.

I learned that Velinda was born and raised in Charlotte, NC and had gone to college in Ohio. A proud African American, she became active in the civil rights movement there.

Velinda and her counterpart in Denver, a Hispanic male, had worked together for ten years, profitably managing the life-events product lines for this large insurance and finance company.

Velinda was accustomed to getting new "up-and-comer bosses" regularly. She had three bosses before her current one, and she always achieved high scores and excellent recommendations. Every year her team grew the business, hit the numbers, and exceeded the target goals. The lawyers, accountants, and agents recommending their products had nothing but compliments and praise for this well-coordinated, mutually supportive team.

As we walked, I observed Velinda and listened to her stories, I began to wonder, *why did Marcia send me here? This woman has it all going on! She's great!*

Velinda, as I suspected, was a natural for the customer-facing unit that required diplomacy, communication skills, and quick thinking. When I learned that Velinda's new boss was a finance person, accustomed to internal audits, paperwork, and reports, I got a hint of why there was a problem brewing.

When I was introduced to Velinda's new boss, I saw a woman of about 5'6" tall with brownish/reddish mousy hair. The auditor energy of control and introspection echoed in her conservative, quiet clothing. I thought, *why is this person in a customer-facing department?* And I questioned how this move, to supervise this department would actually even help this woman's career. But, Velinda was my client (not her boss), so I put those thoughts away.

Marcia had told Velinda that I was there as a coach to help her develop skills to improve the relationship with her new boss. I remember thinking that Velinda didn't need me; her boss probably did! But Marcia wanted to know why a stellar performing department for over ten years, was suddenly looking like it was heading toward a crash and burn, so here I was, tasked to figure out the how and why, and then work to resolve whatever issue was at the root.

Cubical. Cubical. Cubical. Rows of cubicles. Nice, for sure, but not very private. Velinda led me into a room at the end of a hallway. There were no windows. I squinted for a moment to get accustomed to the extremely antiseptic fluorescent lighted room, straight out of a science fiction movie. Was someone going to strap me down to the single table in the middle of the room? The table and a few chairs were the only furnishings and color in the whole room. A single telephone sat in the middle of the table, and cell phone signals did not work in this room, I was told. Once I got the flashes of horror movie/ police drama inquisitions out of my head, I faced Velinda and began the interview in earnest.

Velinda opened the meeting by saying she was glad the company was investing in her. But she was also curious as to why, at this stage of her career, she'd want to go through coaching.

I explained to Velinda that my job was to help her navigate this situation, where it seemed that she and her boss were not getting along.

Once I assured Velinda that our conversations would be held in confidence, she transformed! Velinda shifted her head back and forth, did a bit of a neck roll, put her hand on her hip, and practically spat out, "She's a racist pig and I'm not going to tolerate her disrespect!" And there it was. Out on the stark table. I was shocked by this sudden change in Velinda.

I had witnessed Velinda's skill at switching communication styles several times based on whom she was speaking to as we moved through the building and arrived at this point. Velinda was the right personality for a client-facing position—able to become whatever someone needed. It was remarkable. She was effortlessly engaging, relatable to a variety of people, and encouraging to others all at the same time. Clearly, she had learned how to be adaptable, sense the needs of others, and connect in a way that made them feel trusted. It didn't make sense that she didn't use those skills to solve this problem with her boss (even if her boss was racist).

Velinda might never have opened up like that, if I was not also African American. The true reason for the conflict between the two women who had to work together would never have been known. Who knows what would have happened to either career? However, in this case, the truth came out and the next steps were to decide how to manage the situation.

THE LAST STRAW

It was a Wednesday when Velinda's boss decided to observe a routine call with a client being conducted by Velinda and one of her staff members, Amy. They were meeting with Mike, a divorce attorney representing a client with an account at Velinda's company.

Divorce is a "life-changing" incident and falls into Velinda's purview. When a couple decides to get a divorce, their assets have to be accounted for, and a determination is made regarding who gets what. Velinda's goal was to do everything possible to make sure attorneys for both parties recommended leaving or opening a new account with her company after the divorce finalized. Velinda and her team had a successful track record. Having worked with Mike before, Velinda knew his aggressive style, his need to win, and she believed he trusted her.

Mike was asking for a few things beyond the normal guidelines, which could potentially anger the opposing counsel. His request would cost Velinda's company a bit more, but Velinda thought there was a way to satisfy both parties.

When he started making his demands, Velinda listened, reminded him of the guidelines, and then said, "Let me see what I can do for you, Mike."

Velinda said she was about to end the call when her boss jumped in and said, "Mike, we can't do that! It's against policy."

Velinda was stunned. She knew that comment would burn Mike, and it did. Over the next twenty minutes, they went back and forth. At the end of the call, Velinda walked out, leaving her boss in the room with Amy.

Velinda exploded in frustration on her call with me. "What was she thinking? Everything was under control till she opened her mouth. I'm the expert here. Why couldn't she just keep her mouth shut and let me do my job! Now I've got this mess to clean up... not to mention how it looks to Mike. This is the kind of stuff she does all the frickin' time. She treats me like I'm an imbecile when she knows nothing about this area, what we do, and how important relationships are in this business!" Velinda concluded.

I asked, "Was your boss right?"

Velinda responded "Technically, yes. What Mike asked for was outside the policy we wrote. What Mike was asking wasn't illegal or anything like that. It was doable. It wouldn't hurt us, and we would gain in the end. You have to understand people like Mike.

He thinks of himself as a 'big man.' Somebody who can make things happen for his clients. He's also quite successful as a divorce and estate attorney. Many of his clients are our clients. He and I have worked together for years. In the end, he always does the right thing for me and his clients. But he also likes to brag about how 'he made the company give in.' So, I play the game. Sometimes we can do it and sometimes we can't. That's not the point. What's important is that my team and I work to give people what they need to the best of our ability. We are not just stewarding the money; we are in the relationship business. That's how we maintain and GROW OUR NUMBERS. That's the bottom line, and she doesn't get it! Now I'm supposed to clean up this mess or eat the consequences, 'cause she's the boss... She gets to make me look bad... to work harder than necessary... and jeopardize my team's work record... Hell NO!"

Velinda was still spinning when I said, "There's another way to look at this."

Velinda snapped, nearly yelling, "What am I supposed to do? Bow down and say yessa massa, no sir massa, of course, you know best massa! until she leaves?"

I let her go on for a few minutes until finally the wind was out of her. I could almost visualize Velinda in her office dropping into a chair, folding her arms across her chest, and waiting for me to react and respond.

"Now that that's out, what do you think was her motivation for speaking up?" I said calmly.

"To undermine me! To make me look stupid! Hell, she's a racist. How should I know? Don't you always say, 'Can't read minds. Don't act like it!' "

"Yep, and what's driving your thinking is two things," I coached.

- You believe she is a racist, but what if she's clueless to the impact of her behavior? What if she is bad at reading the room and connecting with people?

- You haven't decided to use your skills to change the dynamics between the two of you.

I continued, "We've talked about this before. We are all thought leaders. Being a thought leader isn't about a title, position, fame, or role. Being a thought leader means framing or reframing the problem so others see the full picture and then encouraging them to take the action necessary to solve the problem. Right now, your opinion that she is a racist is stopping you from using your gifts and talents. What were you thinking when she was in the room? Is it possible that you are really mad because you didn't shut her down?"

Velinda was quiet.

I continued, "We've discussed the impact of a new player being introduced to a team, how it always changes the group dynamics and the storming stage that is coming, and the effort it takes to build trust. Sooner or later tension builds, tempers fly, and the new person becomes the bad guy. You have to decide: Step up or step away."

"It's not my job to educate her. She's the VP, not me!" Velinda spat out.

"Then who suffers if you don't step up? If you choose not to step in and use your skills to guide the situation, then you've decided to accept whatever happens. What do you think that means for you, your team, and for your department's stated mission to serve people in their time of need?"

Velinda was silent. A few seconds later she said, "I need to think about this. It's time for me to go."

Several days later, Velinda's boss was observing an email chain from a client who seemed to be irate, ranting and raving about a situation with a policy. Velinda and her counterpart in Denver were letting the person vent, waiting to see what the real issue was, before jumping in. They'd gone through this before and were adept at handling the situation in due time. Her boss tried to resolve the issue immediately and got things really confused and more muddled than before. At the next team meeting, her boss said, "You people can't make a decision! You can't get anything right without help!" to a department that had been excelling for years at this job!

At our next session, I reminded Velinda that this white woman had never worked with minorities before. She most likely did not know she was triggering emotions with words she was using insensitively.

"Velinda, I'll grant you she may be racist, but she's a benevolent racist. Benevolent racists are uninformed people who are culturally unaware of the history and sensitivities of other races, ethnic, or social groups," I said.

During the call, I was able get Velinda to the point where she could suspend judgment about the intentions of her boss and entertain the possibility that she was unintentionally pitching these bombs. Velinda asked me to help her uncover if her boss was really racist or clueless. By the end of the call, Velinda was comfortable that she could talk to her boss about work and gingerly request permission to talk about their relationship.

When Velinda's boss granted permission, Velinda took a deep breath and asked, "Do you trust me?"

Her boss looked at her and said, "No. And if we're being honest, I don't think you trust me either."

Velinda said she was a bit taken back. After a moment, she thought, *Well it's out there. Neither of us trusts the other person.* My words were ringing in Velinda's head. *Ask for permission to give tough feedback first; otherwise it hurts, shuts the other person down, and you perpetuate the distrust.*

"You are right. Would you like to know why?" Velinda thought her boss had a smug look on her face and her first instinct was to knock it off. Velinda said it was all she could do to stay focused on what we had practiced.

"Sure" was her boss's response.

"You may not know it, but you use phases that are offensive to and demeaning to Black people. Did you know that I feel like you don't like me because of my color?"

Velinda told me afterwards, "The woman turned beet red!" I thought she was going to throw up or cry, but she didn't. She just sat there." Velinda gave her boss a couple of examples, including the latest one using the phrase "you people can't do anything right."

When it was all over, Velinda knew that her boss had no clue about how hurtful and inappropriate her words had been. It was clear to Velinda that her boss was appalled to be thought of as someone who would say or do anything deliberately hostile.

"What now?" Velinda wanted to know. Her boss didn't apologize. Should she be upset?

I suggested that Velinda go back to focusing on the work. "Your boss is probably not going to say anything. She needs time to process this, and the last thing she'll want to do is make another mistake. After being told she was being hurtful, she's likely not going to do or say anything that could be interpreted that way again. Give her a little time," I urged Velinda. "You may not get an apology at this point. And truthfully, it may never happen. Then again, you may get it. But more than likely the fact that she made that big a mistake would be horrific to her and would leave her feeling awkward, afraid, and alone."

We talked about how it's natural for the boss to wonder if she had said all the wrong things before. This could leave her unable to communicate. That the way to get her re-engaged was to keep talking to her about the work for now. "It will keep you both in a safe zone," I said.

I suggested that Velinda stick her head in her boss's office and tell that she was there to help the boss be successful. That she wanted to create a relationship where the two of them could work together.

By the end of the six months, I had taught Velinda how to open up and then close down discussions in a positive way. By stepping in when the timing was right and adapting her style repeatedly, trust between them improved. Working together they learned how to use their different viewpoints productively and allow each other to play to their strengths.

A year later, Velinda worked with her boss to complete a redesign project in order to improve their department's workflow. This project was a priority for Velinda's boss. Velinda was okay with this project because she learned how to manage up, to see beyond the current day, and to forecast changes that were going to affect the business.

Velinda's boss began to depend on Velinda to help her understand how she came across and how to better engage others, especially around tough conversations. Velinda learned more about process improvements and enriched her strategic thinking skills.

They were both sad when her boss was tapped to move on. Eighteen months prior, Velinda's boss was trying to get Velinda fired, and Velinda was about to file discrimination charges. But, after six months of working with me, they developed a great rapport and working relationship. Velinda got the high-value projects. She got to be the leader in presenting new ideas and recommendations, and it was a better working environment for the whole team in the end.

REMARKABLE LEADERSHIP LESSONS

- **Agree to Work Together:** Even before identifying the opportunity for improvement and development, make sure it's something everyone wants to work on and sees the value in. Being a leader is hard work and even though everyone can lead, not everyone wants to lead.
- **Agree to Regular Meetings:** Today, many companies allow people to schedule meetings on anyone's calendar without asking for permission first. This open scheduling system creates

challenges and goes against best practices for working. Blocking time on another person's calendar sends a clear signal that this time was deemed important and for that person's benefit. Managers who regularly bump development time with their people send a signal that this is not a priority to that manager. It doesn't matter if there's a good reason to reschedule. It you look back over your calendar for the last three months and you've rescheduled more than 20 percent of your meetings, re-evaluate the time and importance of messages you're sending to your team members.

- **Listen well:** I find meeting on the phone has significant advantages. My clients often lose themselves in thought and say things they wouldn't say in person. I find I can hear what isn't said and ask questions to bring out what should have been said— but wasn't. Learning to listen well is a skill. Asking compelling, thought-provoking questions is a skill. Finding the courage to inquire is a choice.

- **Presenting problems vs. the root cause:** Identifying what's not working isn't as obvious as asking the person what's happened. We all start with statements that describe what's happened and the events that have taken place. Typically, people easily describe "what should have happened." However, many times the root cause is found when we examine what we expected to happen and why. Questions in this area will give rise to the stories we tell ourselves, the judgments we make, and how our past experiences define what we expect in the present.

PROFILE: SPOTTING A BAD LEADER

DENISEism:
Everybody has good and bad in them.
It's human to believe that if you are like me,
you'll act like me, you'll understand me.

A major media company invited me to speak to their minority diversity committee. Lucas was among the fifty people there. Lucas is black, about 5'9", in his forties, and a Baptist-raised Midwesterner from Ohio. He was full of swagger and used his attractiveness as an asset. Stylishly put together, he carried himself with an energy that was a cross between playful, creative, and a "man with a bullhorn and clipboard to get-sh*t-done-or-get-outta-my'way' personality.

Lucas was an employee on the production crews. He did all kinds of television shows. Primarily in the housing, decorating, design kind of space, before shows like HGTV got to be as big as they are. Lucas handled staging and other behind-the-scenes work that got the shows on the air, looking great. He was a production genius. Three of his mega projects won national awards.

In addition to staging, Lucas worked with film and did some editing. He had moved into a full-time job and then, when ownership of the company changed, he was laid off.

At that point Lucas decided he wanted to go across the country to California. He thought that with his award-winning television credentials, he would be in the perfect place to find a dream job. He wanted to be more "out" than he could be in Ohio and thought the LA gay community would embrace and support him. He stayed out in LA until he realized that he wasn't getting any traction, because LA is a place that is all about who you know, and he didn't "know" anybody. He's a Midwesterner.

Meantime, he was receiving reports that his mother was ill back home in Ohio, and his dad was also getting sick and probably wouldn't be able to care for his wife. There was drama swirling throughout the family in Ohio. No one was telling him specifically what was going on. So, Lucas made the decision to go back home for a year. He figured he could nurse his mother back to good health, get his siblings to share responsibilities for their parents, and then he could move on.

When he got back to Ohio, Lucas saw that his sister was not stepping up. She was busy with her own challenges and had no capacity to care for their mother, as her own son was a teenager getting into gangs and other questionable stuff. His brother was not stepping up either.

Neither sibling nor his parents could tell Lucas what was wrong with Mom, but he could see with his own eyes that she was not the same woman he knew. Once Lucas was able to visit with doctors with his mother and father, they received the results of some tests. The tests came back with a diagnosis of early to moderate stages of Alzheimer's disease. His mom was exhibiting signs of dementia, and it was only going to get worse. He had to make a decision: Follow his heart, or stay in Ohio to care for his parents.

Lucas thought, *this is just another project. Once I get mother stable, then I can go on with my own life.* It didn't work out that way, so eventually he realized he had to get a job. Lucas's father was an elected official and very well known, so Lucas took a job with the county government. Now, here's Lucas, a highly creative guy with a good bent toward implementation, heading off to work in a government bureaucracy. He can walk into a room and redesign it in his head in minutes. His aesthetic sense is off the chart. Implementation skills, also off the chart. He's a bing, bing, bing into action organizer who had done award-winning projects in the creative world of film and television. Sharp, sharp, sharp, and now in county government. I just knew there was going to be an issue here the minute I heard where Lucas was working!

When asked to describe Dan, his boss, Lucas said that he was a black man in his fifties, supervising five people in the department. The other people in the department included a thirty-year-old white male, a twenty-eight-year-old Iranian female (who had issues with the boss because she was a practicing Muslim), a twenty-nine-year-old white female, and a fifty-year-old white female. The HR business partner was a white female, and the head of HR was a black female.

Lucas told me he needed my help because he was "on warning" at his company, and he didn't understand why. In his mind he just did what Dan asked him to do. But, Lucas shared, his boss wasn't talking to him. And while the boss was not one who actually talked much to anyone in the department, he was particularly and quite obviously NOT talking to Lucas. So, HR got involved.

Lucas said the HR business partner didn't give him a date on when the investigation/probation would be completed. He just wasn't doing well enough was all he knew. Then he remembered HR gave him a write-up that said he had thirty days to respond to the inquiry/investigation/complaint. He hadn't called me when he got the write-up. When I questioned him, as the days were counting down until he was supposed to respond to the write-up, Lucas shared the content of the complaint documents, finally.

Lucas was distraught, talking 500 words a minute and only giving me bits and pieces of what happened. From what I could make out, Lucas didn't have any measurable performance indicators at all.

They were looking for Lucas to come to work on time and clock out. Okay. You've got to check in with Dan. Okay. Nothing that would say, fire this man or put him on performance review. I was curious as to what was really going on and knew there must be more to the story that was being left unsaid. It seemed that perceptions and bad management were the issues to explore.

Even though Lucas was liked by his coworkers, he didn't know to whom he could turn to for help. In fact, Lucas told me one of the issues in this complaint against him was that he talked too much to people. "You're disrupting the team," they had told him.

Aha, I thought. *Could it be Lucas was telling someone too much? Did something get back to the boss that was seen as a breach of confidentiality?*

Lucas was told he couldn't keep his phone on his desk. He told them he had to have it on because of his mother with Alzheimer's. "I have to be reachable if her doctor or the nursing home needs me," he told them. I asked Lucas if HR told him about FMLA? [Family Medical Leave Act]

"No," he said.

"Have they advised you on acceptable ways of how to stay available in an emergency?"

"No," he answered.

I surmised from our discussion that Lucas was pretty much on his own and had not been supported by HR. Had he gone through training on procedures? He said, "Not really."

Lucas had taken the training, but the system he learned didn't actually work the way the training material detailed. Lucas told the IT people and his boss that the system wasn't working, and got the cold shoulder after that. I assessed it was probably the "little things" that pushed his boss to believe Lucas was insubordinate and a disruptor in his nice, peaceful department. But, because of Lucas's political connections, Dan couldn't fire him without serious provocation. Both he and Lucas had to follow the process.

In preparation for the hearing, Lucas and I talked about what would be discussed. We went over, line by line, all of the issues described in the PIP[1].

After reviewing the PIP, it was time to talk strategy. I explained:

- It was critical that Lucas come across as professional but not defensive.
- Wait to answer the questions from the arbitrator.
- Be truthful. If you did it, say so. If you didn't do it, say so.
- When you feel like everyone is against you, take three deep breaths. Remember, no matter what happens, you're going to be fine.

I recommended that he go into the meeting, smile, maintain a good disposition, treat the meeting like he was trying to find out more information, be curious about why he was even there, and ask questions to clarify their understanding of acceptable performance.

Lucas was honest about what transpired at the meeting. Afterwards, Lucas and I worked together to construct a letter rebutting the complaints. When Lucas arrived at work the following Monday, he sent the letter to the hearing officer. About a week later he got the response.

The hearing officer determined, "You admitted in the meeting that these things actually occurred therefore you will take a one day suspension." And then the officer continued, "However, your boss could not explain just what was expected of you and I believe that this was a contributing factor to the situation." And that was the end of that.

Resigned to the consequences, Lucas shared, "I hate this job, 'cause I'm in the wrong job. I need to be here for my mom. I need to be here for my dad." This happens to lots of people. They carry

---

[1] Performance Improvement Plan

"life" with them around work and into relationships with coworkers, supervisors, subordinates, and all the internal and external clients.

I recommended that going forward Lucas needed to document everything he worked on, time stamp it, send it in email, and ALWAYS ask exactly what is expected of him. "You put a read receipt on that son of a gun," I told him with a grin.

Lucas called me a few days later. Dan was avoiding him again.

I told him, "Ask for a meeting. I suggest you find out why Dan is avoiding you and treating you like you stole something." I told Lucas to meet with his boss face-to-face because there seemed like an underlying issue was still disrupting the working relationship. I advised him to look at Dan and say, "I had the expectation that when I completed the disciplinary action, I would have a clean slate. You're not talking to me, you're avoiding me, and I don't understand how we're going to go forward if you're not gonna give me a clean slate."

After meeting with Dan, Lucas called me back and said Dan's eyes almost popped out of his face when Lucas confronted him. Dan, communication-challenged, said he assumed that Lucas wouldn't want to talk to him at all since Dan had Lucas up on disciplinary action. Lucas told him he simply wanted to know what Dan needed so he wouldn't have to guess and do the wrong thing, thereby causing ripple effects of problems. They agreed to communicate better regarding expectations and deadlines.

I asked Lucas, "What did you learn from this?"

Lucas answered, "You were right. I should have nipped this in the bud earlier. I should have asked what was going on and asked to talk about it. There's something else I didn't tell you...."

I said, "What was that?"

Lucas said that after he left the meeting with Dan, Sam (the white guy on the team) came to him and said, "Lucas, I'm really sorry. I knew Dan was giving you a hard time. I knew that he was intentionally trying to get you out. I should have stepped up and said something and I didn't."

Lucas learned from Sam that Dan had a reputation for punishing his subordinates if they crossed him. Lucas was made into an example for the department, and this reinforced the fear held by the team members to comply with Dan's demands... or else.

Lucas shared that Sam claimed it wasn't anything Lucas had actually done. "But," Sam continued, "what you don't understand is that what everybody knows now is that Dan just doesn't like men who are gay."

In all probability, Dan most likely had a story or reason for using punishment as a motivator for everyone in the department. Sam's "confidential" chat uncovered more than Dan's feelings about how he felt about Lucas's sexual preferences. The story is an indication of Dan's need for control, conformity, and dominance.

REMARKABLE LEADERSHIP LESSONS

- **Judgment that leads to discrimination and unfair treatment is an equal opportunity phenomenon.** Doesn't matter if the person is black/white/purple, whatever, everyone has unconscious biases or myths that influence our actions but often go unrecognized. Assuming we all think, believe, and will act the same way on its face seems silly. Yet we surround ourselves with people just like us, who think like us, want the same things we want, and cast out of our circle those who don't. Those with title and power can hide behind policies and procedures to force their beliefs on others. Few executives have the wherewithal to regularly examine how culture is shaped by the policies, our unconscious biases and myths. Even fewer are willing to admit that their culture—how we work together and what we tolerate from each other in the name of fairness, creates and sustains a system of unfair treatment based upon how one looks, acts, background and socioeconomic status. When we are blind to the possibility that discrimination exists in our businesses, then we are tolerating its existence in the world.

- **If you're poorly trained, you're poorly trained.** Expect that your boss is more than likely poorly trained. HR regularly presents a distribution of performance ratings at the end of the year. When you think of the "bell curve," remember that 50 percent performed at or above, and that 50 percent performed at or below. You've got the same odds of getting a decent to great boss as you do of getting an inept and just plain bad boss.

- **Never underestimate the drain from the "slog."** Doing what has to be done and delaying doing what you believe you are meant to do is HARD. Over time, you not only lose your way, but if you don't pay attention, you'll lose your fire and it will wear you out.

- **Find something you can be passionate about within your situation.** Your energy, ability to focus, and that sense of accomplishment changes when you're not working on your passion or seeing results in areas important to you. Connect your assignment with your values. Understanding why you're stuck in a dead-end job may give you a reason for staying stuck, but it doesn't feed your soul.

- **When you've been thrown a curve ball...** It is so easy to get derailed. When life throws you a curve ball, make sure you have a plan to re-evaluate your goals. If you decide to take care of someone who is critically ill, get connected with a support network and then re-evaluate your career options based on the time and focus you believe you'll be able to realistically commit. The most wonderful thing is that you don't have to work in a job you hate or one that drains you. Find someone who can help you close past chapters in your life, reassess your skills and passions, and then begin anew with an inspiring new end-goal in mind. Reinvention is a gift. Embrace it now, and it will serve you well in the future.

PROFILE: THE COURAGE TO NAVIGATE GENDER POLITICS— LEADING AND MENTORING WOMEN

DENISEism:
Sitting on the fence gets you nowhere.

Arlen and I were attending the same local networking event. Our eyes met across the room and a flicker of a question passed over Arlen's face. As he approached, he extended his hand a bit tentatively. We exchanged a firm handshake, and as we declared our names, a brilliant, warm smile illuminated his face. Arlen leaned in just a bit and asked me if we had met before. "Your face seems so familiar. I attend these events regularly. Have you been here before?"

"No, not really," I answered. "Most of my business isn't here in Charlotte, so I don't get to many events here. I decided to attend this one because of the topic—HR metrics. Dr. Mark Huselid is the speaker, and I've been a fan since the 90s. His work became the foundational thinking for the organizational development work I did at Monsanto, and later at the Gap."

As I was talking, I did an instantaneous, subconscious, mental *first impression* assessment of my new contact. Arlen was about 5'9" with graying, dark brown hair. His dark blue suit was well made and loose fitting. His jacket hung open where I noticed the beginnings of a belly about to start hanging over his belt. Arlen wasn't particularly handsome. His eyes were brown and close set. His hair, a bit unkempt, was cut long on the sides, and I could see the beginnings of a comb over. Arlen had an inviting smile and dimples set into pallid cheeks. Just an average-looking man who had seen hard times and lived to tell about it.

As Arlen shared his mutual interest in the HR topic, and his role managing projects at a bank, he was still trying to place where he'd met me. Arlen started listing a few places where we could have run into each other. When he mentioned an event he attended the previous year with his wife ("What about SEED20?"), a light bulb illuminated.

"Yep! That's it!"

As we continued to talk and laugh, we realized that I knew Arlen's wife, Eve. She and I had met just before I started my business. Eve was one of a number of people who enrolled in a class, *The Right Fit*, and were there to learn why they felt they didn't fit in their current job.

Several weeks after the networking event, Arlen called and asked to meet with me confidentially. We met at a small, private coffee shop in the south end of Charlotte. I'd arrived before Arlen and when he came in, he wasn't smiling. He looked lost in thought.

Arlen filled in the details on his team at the project management office and confided that, while he loved his work, managing people was getting the best of him. I asked if there was anyone in particular about whom he was concerned.

Arlen was finding that although the company had purchased the latest project management tools, it was difficult getting people to use them. The software would give senior management visibility to what was going on with projects. They wanted to use the information to be proactive; to better manage estimate resources needed, and to implement new initiatives.

About six months prior, he had posted an opening for a senior project manager, and interviewed three really good candidates. His team liked them, and the recruiter was pushing for Arlen to make a decision. At the last minute, Arlen's HR contact said he had to interview Susan, an internal candidate.

At first, he didn't think much of it because HR said he could still hire the best person regardless, but as a company, they wanted to give internal staff as much opportunity for advancement as possible.

After speaking with Susan, Arlen told HR he had reservations about hiring her. Susan didn't seem to take accountability for things, and there were gaps in her understanding about project management. The biggest issue was her answers to the questions about herself. Arlen, like many managers, asks everyone, "What are your strengths and biggest weaknesses? And how do they contribute to your success?" Susan rambled on about her technical skill strength and revealed that her biggest weakness was something about overcommitting and then working hard to meet her commitments. She rattled on about how people don't appreciate when you do things for them or that they don't keep their word. Arlen thought it wouldn't be a good fit.

When he spoke to HR, suddenly he discovered that he had no choice; he had to fill the open spot with Susan. "I was new, and my boss thought it was a good idea to take her too. He said I could manage around her," Arlen explained.

"Then," Arlen continued, "a few weeks after Susan came onboard, I had lunch with her old boss and found out she didn't really get along with anyone in his department. No one wanted to work with her because she was always throwing them under the bus. Her projects often missed key milestones but somehow, she did finish them. There were comments about the quality of her work and how she adjusted the plan, which was why her performance ratings were only 'meets expectations.'" And now, here was Arlen telling me that Susan, now a senior project manager on *his* team, was struggling to keep up with the work.

I had a feeling that there was more to the story and asked, "So what haven't you mentioned?"

Arlen changed the subject. "Tell me about you and how you work."

"Well, you've spent a lot of time learning about the technical aspects of your job, right?" Arlen nodded. "What's the difference between a good performer and a great one?"

"Well, a good performer gets the job done; a great one has something extra. They get the job done but there's something about them. I know it when I see it," Arlen answered thoughtfully.

"What would it mean to you if you knew exactly what that 'something extra' was and could teach your team how to use that 'something extra' to their advantage?" I went on to explain, "I'm really good at helping people understand the difference and then to be able to describe it well. If you can't describe it, it can't be done. I teach executives and HR how to create a culture of high performance. We work together to enhance a person's soft skills, which take a person's performance from mediocre, to good, then on to great. My clients learn how to lead, inspire, and build sustainable work habits that lead to better and better performance. What I'm really good at is helping people think clearly, and figuring out how to deal with the emotional and political landscape at work that stops executives from being effective."

I leaned forward and asked Arlen, "So what's getting in the way of you being more effective?"

Arlen lowered his voice, moved closer to me and said, "My wife says you are confidential. I mean like in a vault. Is that right?"

"Yes!" I affirmed.

Arlen took a deep breath and let out a huge sigh. At that moment, I felt the tension leave his whole body as he started describing the last six months with Susan on his team.

"Susan just seems tense and wound up tight as a drum all the time. She walks into a room and everyone gets tense. When she talks to you, it feels like she's berating you. She always has to make THE point. Even when she says nice things, you just don't feel good about it. Everyone senses it, and we speak in whispers about it when she's not around. I mean, how do you tell someone to chill out?"

I interrupted, "You mean how does a man tell a woman 'chill out?'" Arlen scoffed and I continued, "One of the unintended consequences of the fifty years of diversity and inclusion efforts in the workplace is that everyone is now more sensitive, feeling uncertain, and suspicious. Men (white men in the good ol' boy network in particular), don't want to say the wrong thing for fear of being called out."

"Are you feeling like you can't talk about her performance?" I asked.

Arlen shared some thoughts on Susan's performance issues. Her meetings were incomplete and frustrating everyone. Because Susan's internal partners weren't filling her in on what was going on, the updates she gave management and the rest of her internal clients were missing critical information, or changes that affected the work product. This information gap was causing Susan's internal clients to have to change their priorities, miss their own deadlines, and then face the backlash from their own directs and supervisors. Senior management was frustrated. Both Arlen and Susan were taking the heat since much of the project was in the red.

When Arlen tried to talk to Susan to understand what was going on, she became defensive and blamed all the problems on her lack of authority to hold her internal partners accountable for staying abreast of the updates and commitments.

As Arlen pressed Susan about her work, he said all she seemed to do was send out more and more emails, and instant messages as the only solution. He'd asked her to set up a meeting with key internal clients to talk with them, and these meetings seemed to get cancelled and were not rescheduled.

The meetings with Susan had become so tense that Arlen stopped talking to Susan and just started working around her. This in turn made Susan more defensive and gave her a new target—Arlen. During their weekly meetings, Susan talked about being overworked and not getting any help. Arlen reassigned her workload to others, hoping she could focus on her key projects. It backfired.

The rest of the team didn't want to work with her either, and rumors were going around that the only reason Susan got the job was because she had "something on somebody." They resented doing her work on top of their own. There were arguments about who was in charge and who could make the final decision on what was going to be done. They reported Susan was "bossing them around," even though the project was reassigned to them and she didn't own the work any longer. Meetings were tense and feelings were raw.

Lowering his head and voice ever so slightly, Arlen shared that HR said this was Susan's last chance. Susan's last boss didn't provide truthful performance reviews. Apparently, when the last boss spoke to Susan, she always had a reasonable explanation; same was happening with Arlen. She asked people to do work, they said they would, and then they didn't. Susan sent out emails, made phone calls, and then the next deadline would come and the work was either partially completed or not done at all. "HR is pushing me to write her up," Arlen confided. "I feel like I was set up to be the bad guy. Everybody's tap-dancing around the issues but looking to me to pull the trigger."

"What do you want?" I asked.

"Frankly, I like Susan. I think she was overpromoted and now she's in over her head. The few times I can get through to her, she's funny and likable. I can see she's trying but the skill gap is huge, and everyone is just over her attitude and her project being in such terrible shape. I want to help her, but I really don't know how, and if I do this wrong, then it will be bad for my team."

"I don't understand. What do you mean?" I asked.

"Well, here's the thing. The best boss I ever had told me, 'No one ever wins or fails by themselves. A person is a high performer because others kick in and work with them. The opposite is also true. A person fails because others don't pitch in to help. They don't show up when that person needs them most, and then they fail, and everyone goes I told you so.'" My team is failing because of the in-fighting. This is the kind of stuff that kills careers. Senior management will see all of us as incapable and not promotable. I've seen it before. Promising people get sidetracked because they can't lead. They get frustrated because 'somehow' they get the work done but management doesn't promote them. Not because they're poor performers, but because they can't influence others, and develop the relationships that smoothly get the work done.

"Our work is dependent upon our ability to see what's possible, build, maintain, and leverage relationships, and collectively make a difference. Staffers don't have direct control over others. We are dependent on our leadership ability to get work done. If we can't do that, then our department is seen as overhead. We're not able to add value to the business and the department goes away.

"Susan is failing because someone let her down and frankly, I'm afraid the problem is spreading throughout my team," complained Arlen.

I asked, "So why don't you just do what HR has suggested and write her up? That will lead to termination, and wouldn't your problem be solved?"

"I guess I'm worried this will be a black mark on my record, and I don't want to go out like this."

The problem was that Arlen hadn't been true to himself. Arlen had forgotten what his mentor/boss taught him. His team was a group of people who were all focused on their individual needs instead of a common purpose. He thought they knew what it meant to work together to make each other better than the day before.

Susan, he admitted, was likely in the wrong job. She was the wrong fit for the team, but Arlen had never asked her what she wanted or needed to be successful. He, like everyone else, was focused on what was wrong.

I worked with Arlen to map out a three-step process:

1. Talk with Susan to understand her perspective and find out what she needed and wanted to do.
2. Meet with the team to reset and define expectations.
3. Address the disappointment of his internal customers and others who were watching this craziness.

REMARKABLE LEADERSHIP IN ACTION

Step 1: Talk with Susan to understand her perspective and find out what she needed and wanted.

When Arlen tried to talk to Susan in order to understand what was going on, she became defensive and started once again blaming all the problems on her lack of authority to hold her internal partners accountable for staying abreast of the updates and commitments. He listened to her for a few minutes and then redirected her with a focused question.

"Susan, I know what has been happening. What I don't know is what you want and need to *feel* successful? What support do you want from me? What do you think our internal customers need and want from us?"

Arlen said he **could** see the questions knocked her for a loop. She was silent for the first time during the meeting. "I want everyone to like me. I know they don't like me and it's because…" And Susan went off on how she knew "they" were against her.

Arlen interrupted her again, keeping her focused, asking "On a scale of one to ten, with one being 'totally distrustful' and ten being

'I fully believe I've got you,' how much do you trust me?" Susan looked at Arlen like she was sizing him up and contemplating if she wanted to kill him.

"Do you want the truth?" she asked.

"Yes!" Arlen confirmed. "Whatever that means, including if it is a one." Arlen held his breath, hoping it wasn't a one, but recognized that as he and I had discussed, it very well might be so.

"Three," she said.

Arlen sighed and said, "Well I've got a bit of work to do, but all is not lost. What is one thing that would move it from a three to a four?"

Susan looked at him, stunned. He could see that his responsiveness touched her. Arlen told me that for the first time, Susan looked like the fight had been taken out of her. Her shoulders relaxed. Her voice lowered, and quivering, she told him, "I'm not sure. I feel like you and everyone else don't believe I can do the job. I feel like I have to fight to be heard, respected, and treated like I know something. What I want is to be treated with respect, listened to, and allowed to have my suggestions treated like they were good. Every time I meet with the team or our internal customers, they are always talking over me, telling me why my idea won't work, and when I say this is what we need to do, I can see the contempt. No one listens to me, and I just get so mad."

Arlen asked the question again. "What is one thing that would move it from a three to a four?"

Finally, Susan gave him something concrete to work with! "I want you to back me when everyone else doesn't do what they're supposed to do. I need an assistant to help me with the administrative work. As a senior project manager, I shouldn't have to do admin tasks."

Arlen was happy that we had role-played this conversation. Susan did exactly what I said she would do. Blame everyone else and ask for more help, which he couldn't give her.

"Susan," Arlen said patiently. "I can't give you an assistant, but can you tell me more about how I can back you up? What do I need to do or say that would make you feel like I am backing you up?"

"I don't know," Susan answered and drifted back into complaint mode. "What I hate most is no one respects me. They make agreements and then flake. Then when it all falls apart, I'm blamed. I guess you could get the internal clients to do what they said they would do."

"If I openly intervene, then they will not respect you. A big part of the senior project manager role is to influence others to take action. What if I work with you on how you can influence others to do the work? That way when it happens, it will be because they respect you. Will that move the needle on the trust level between us?"

Arlen could see she was confused. It wasn't what she wanted, but he thought it must have struck a chord. "How would that work?" she asked.

Arlen, relieved, saw the first sign that Susan was opening up as she had asked what I had told him was a "possibility question."

REMARKABLE LEADERSHIP MINDSET: POSSIBILITY QUESTIONS

We cannot change anything until we are willing to ponder that things can be different. Possibility questions define a future state: We have to stop looking at what is, start wondering what could be, and ask ourselves what would it take for me to get it done?

Step 2: Meet with the team to reset and define expectations.

Arlen and I designed a special meeting for his team to reset expectations on what it means to be a member of his team. They developed ground rules and agreements describing how to work together in a supportive way.

The main emphasis was for the team to understand that agreeing to something and then not following up or not following through on their word was a problem.

I forewarned Arlen that Susan may not be the only person who was a "bad fit" for the team. Every person has a unique combination of strengths and weaknesses; they also have different motivations and drivers. Each team member sees the world through individual lenses and perspectives, which underpins their thinking on what a good outcome looks like, how they live their values, and what integrity means to them.

Until the formal meeting, Arlen hadn't taken the time to personally understand his direct reports' motivators or passions. He assumed they all knew what it took to be a member of a highly productive team. He assumed they knew that each member would have their own work, their own way of doing things, but that there would also be an expectation of working together, helping, mentoring, sharing their wisdom, or even making sacrifices to ensure that ultimately, the team wins.

Arlen and I also talked about how the HR processes actually drove a wedge in the idea of being a project team. Arlen also admitted that he hadn't been a good leader. He let the current culture—the existing way of doing things—determine what's right instead of setting the vision and defining how he wanted people to work together. He forgot that culture is determined by the leader of the group. Organizations are a bunch of cultures living within and next to other cultures.

Arlen and I planned a one-day team retreat he coined *Project New Beginnings*. While he knew that one day off-site wasn't going to solve all the problems, he had a couple of specific goals and outcomes on his agenda.

At the end of the retreat, his team had ground rules which clearly defined expectations and what to do when things went sideways. In his mind, a good performer was one who delivered on the work and upheld the company values.

Arlen started laying the groundwork for everyone to understand a major indicator of success on his team, was embracing change; that leading and inspiring others to change was as important as completing a project. An outstanding performer (not just "meets expectations") was someone who helped others be successful. Outstanding performers were mentors, thought-leaders, and facilitators of information and skill development. Outstanding performers were able to demonstrate that their projects made a long-term positive impact on others and the business.

Step 3: Address the disappointment of internal customers.

Arlen had to face the reality that the department's internal customers were disappointed with what was being delivered by his team. The company's systems rewarded individual performance at the expense of collaboration. The systems needed to encourage teamwork and being supportive of colleagues to reach the finish line, while delivering excellent work product in order to keep the internal customers happy with Arlen's team.

As it stood, Susan was being blamed exclusively for projects falling off track. As Arlen had been unable to gain agreement from his peers and the senior executives that it was unacceptable for their people to make promises and then not do the work, he needed to change the way he and his team communicated and revamp expectations all the way around.

Arlen collected a list of the internal clients assigned to Susan's projects. He planned to meet with the managers of each one. The goal would be to clear the air and gain help in holding their people accountable, making it clear it was no longer acceptable for them to commit to do things and then not deliver. If they agreed to review requirements by a certain date, they must do it. If not, they had to let Susan know in a timely manner. If they foresaw a potential issue with the schedule, they needed to let Susan know when the schedule was first being created. His management peers were also to check in with their people to make sure all parties were living up to the agreements they made. No surprises!

HR would routinely let him know that someone was complaining about Susan—anonymously. No more! Anyone complaining would need to take responsibility for owning what they were saying. HR should speak directly to Arlen about their concerns regarding Susan or any member of his team. He could only manage the things of which he had knowledge. He also asked HR to coach the people around Susan on being open-minded. I helped Arlen develop a coaching tool for everyone to use.

Susan was initially fearful of all the changes regarding expectations. Arlen liked Susan personally and didn't want to have to fire her. Arlen's fear of failure was clouding his judgment, and the messages from the culture were steering him away from his values.

I was able to quiet Arlen's thoughts of failure and teach him how to train Susan to counteract the habitual thinking pattern of seeing the worst and becoming defensive. As Arlen continued to share his thoughts with Susan, her performance improved over the next eight months, but it took some time for others on the team to really embrace Arlen's vision. Although, several members left the team, Arlen was able to hire new people who were a better fit for the work and culture he was building.

Susan left too. She and Arlen are still talking, and he said she is doing well at her new company. Arlen said Susan's decision to go was probably the right thing, not because she hadn't changed but because there were people in senior management who didn't open up to the possibility that she had changed. She felt a fresh start and leaving on a high note was the right thing for her.

PROFILE: WHEN YOUR BOSS ISN'T A GREAT LEADER

DENISEism:
Taming Attila

If you will, imagine a battlefield with warriors ready to begin combat. On one side, Attila the Hun, with a dark pointy beard and thick mustache, beady menacing eyes, a crown set atop his mesh war head protection, perched high atop his horse, spear raised. Who is he attacking? In this case, Sandra. Bespectacled Sandra with blonde hair neatly styled, 5'6" of debutante Southern style, breeding, and money. Why is Attila attacking Sandra? Because he can. Because he's someone who has a very high need for control, and he takes it by dominating (subtly and sometimes not so subtly by berating or firing people who disagree with him). Sandra is in his chain of command and thus under his perceived control; she is also his target.

When Sandra and her kids were left homeless and penniless by her husband in a boring stereotypical middle-aged crisis "I'm-done with you. I-need-someone, younger/prettier, who-adores-me-more" divorce, Sandra entered the work world. Debutantes are bred to be mothers and run a household. Debs DO charity work;

they are not charity cases! That's what she was taught, but that wasn't her nature.

Sandra definitely needed to earn a living to support her kids, but she still loved helping people and used her volunteer time to work in the mental health area and create scholarships for kids who wanted to go to college. Doing for others was in her blood, and she found the idea of building something from scratch or taking it to the next level appealing.

Sandra and I began working together long before Sandra accepted her current position as VP, Community and Public Affairs, for a locally owned chain of retail stores. The company had been in business over sixty-six years, when Sandra joined the management team.

Upon the company's inception, the founder and the board wanted to give back in the community. The founder's son was a victim of alcohol abuse, and after his son died, his wife became active in Alcoholics Anonymous. She persuaded her husband to set up a philanthropic arm of the business in honor of his son, and it has remained in effect ever since.

Each year the organization awarded grants to nonprofit organizations that helped people deal with chemical addiction. The programs supported by the foundation included addiction prevention and education, and more recently, the board approved funding shelters dedicated to helping women victims of domestic violence and sex trafficking. Sandra was hired to oversee this philanthropic department.

Over the years, the retail company had grown from a few stores to over 200 locations. Sandra said, "People join this company and if they get past being a store clerk, they don't leave. We have great benefits, although the pay is a bit low. I think people stay because it's easy and barely any competition. This company has been able to keep well over 30 percent of the market and has pretty good margins."

The entire management team, except Sandra and the head of HR, grew up within the company. As Sandra got to know them, she found out that they all intended to stay until they could cash in on their retirement.

Getting to know Sandra over the years, I understood that Sandra was focused on her core values. She was a single mother. She read incessantly and talked to various experts to learn and hone a servant leadership philosophy. In her mind, the role of a leader is to serve the needs of those for whom she is responsible.

She believed that having a high engagement score amongst employees was how you knew you had a financially successful AND socially conscious business. It was the duty of the management team to make sure employees were doing the right things in the right order. Sandra read the latest studies on the impact of employee engagement and customer retention, and she wanted to work for a company that made it work. Working with a management team that understood that customer satisfaction (and ultimately retention) was tied to how you treat employees, was at the top of her bucket list.

The organization's management team was comprised of three women and three men. She was ultimately hired by the CEO, Greg. He was a 5'4", don't-rock-the-boat-or-I'll-make-your-life-miserable, sturdily built white man born and bred in the area, who had been with the company for thirty-three years. He started as a clerk and worked his way up to VP of Operations, where he had remained for nearly seventeen years.

During the initial interview, Greg bragged about how they still worked 9 to 5 with one hour off for lunch, cluing Sandra in on the culture.

The Grant Program was something that Sandra's boss didn't want to have to manage so he had been looking for someone to take it over, upgrade it, and make sure the money was being spent wisely. In the past, Sandra had made use of services of various local nonprofits to get through tough times when support from her ex wasn't available. Sandra's children were entering high school and her ex-husband wasn't always forthcoming with the child support payments. A job working in nonprofit was initially thrilling, and the fact that her position came with a sizable increase over her previous salary made it seem like this new job was a dream come true. With reasonable hours, a good salary, a pension, 401K, and a car, Sandra was too starry-eyed to recognize that she was stepping into a case of, *if it seems to be too good to be true, then it is.*

It wasn't long before she realized that Greg's primary goal was to look good to the board of directors, and that meant making money. His preferred method of increasing the revenue line was cost cutting and penny pinching. People suggested ways to increase revenue by adding new services, targeted marketing to high-volume customers, only to be told it wouldn't work and would cost too much money to implement.

Sandra was able to improve efficiency in the grant process to ensure that grant recipients were accountable for the funds they were given. Rubber stamping grants to the same applicants year after year was eliminated. Ineffective or inefficient use of the funds meant the grant would be awarded to a more deserving applicant. The board was impressed with the tracking status reports and the end results of Sandra's work. Greg didn't pay much attention to the nonprofit side as long as it didn't raise any eyebrows. Sandra was responsible for the community grants, as well as public relations and marketing.

Within a year, Sandra realized that Greg's leadership style was on par with Attila the Hun. His top down management style was so controlling, it was causing front-line employees to leave. The flow of applicants was drying up because the company's reputation was suffering.

For example, Greg had cameras installed in the hallways so he could see who was coming and going and when people came back from lunch. Store employees were working seventeen-hour days, and many of the stores were short-staffed while headquarters staff averaged forty hours a week.

When the VP of Operations, who was hired more than fifteen years prior, brought new ideas to Greg, he quickly shot them down, and would overrule her on every decision. Repeatedly reminding her that, after all, he had done her job and wrote all the procedures that were in place currently. Who better to know how things should be run than the person who wrote the procedures?

Greg was equally hard-nosed on HR. He came down hard when too much was spent on overtime. The previous HR manager was a woman with no experience in HR. But Greg and she had an affair, and then they decided to get married. She later resigned when the board heard about their relationship. In her place, Greg hired a person with no senior management experience. She was quite capable of sustaining the HR function but inexperienced in retail and anything beyond the transactional responsibilities. She too found it nearly impossible to make any changes without Greg getting angry. The only time she was able to make a change was if the laws changed. She was overwhelmed with recruiting most of the time. The initial training programs, written by Greg and his wife, were poorly done and inadequate for changing market conditions.

The only people to whom Greg seemed to give a pass were his buddies; the heads of safety and finance. They also happened to be men.

A new member was appointed to the board with retail industry expertise. She began talking about how retail was changing and strongly suggested that although competition may not be a motivating factor, evolving customer expectations were, and it was time for this sleepy little company to wake up.

As the board member began to bring more and more evidence that improvements could result in higher revenues, lower costs, and improved productivity, the chairman of the board put pressure on Greg to explore the new ideas.

Under this pressure, Greg was in Sandra's office trying to convince her to be the lead on the continuous improvement project.

He offered Sandra the added responsibilities and she was told that her partners on this venture were the other two women, the VP Operations and the HR Director. Together, they would work on this "important board-initiated project." When Sandra pushed back, asking why the VP Operations wasn't leading the team, Greg used his fake flattering tactic, saying, "You like this stuff, and this will be good for your development. I mean, you've been asking for a bigger role, haven't you?" With that he pushed back his chair and stood.

As he came around the desk to leave the office, Sandra asked, "So what's the budget and timeframe for this?"

He turned and said, "No budget. I just want you to explore options. Get me something in a few months."

When Sandra met with me to discuss taking on this additional responsibility, she was torn. On one hand, the idea of leading the effort was exciting, might lead to more responsibility in operations and a raise. From the work she did on upgrading the grant administration, Sandra had gotten a bug for design thinking. She thought the idea of finally getting to help employees do their job better was exciting and full of possibilities. On the other hand, it was Greg, and she knew he was only doing this to show the board how well he was running the company, as is. What would he do to throw a wrench into the program once it was up and running?

I cautioned her that while a larger role and a salary increase might happen eventually, we needed to begin with a strategy to engage the other two women assigned to this project. There was a good chance they too would see through Greg's ploy to appease the board and conclude, "why even try?"

SUSPICION, JEALOUSY, AND COMPETITION

Sandra had learned to bring her proposals to Greg with the financials included as a key portion of her presentations. She made her explanations about how any new request/process was in his best interest. Over the three years, Sandra was able to deliver on her goals to modernize the foundation's activities. As a result of her innovations, she was asked to consult with other grant foundations in the area, which made their organization and Attila look good.

As Sandra became better at rejecting attacks from Attila and coming out as the winner of more and more battles, she started running into issues with her female peers. There was resentment and even cold-shoulder hostility. How was Sandra getting everything she wanted or needed while they were still struggling and being attacked all the time?

At lunch one day, the VP of Operations made a thinly veiled accusation of Sandra being, "the Golden Child." Sandra felt the backroom snide questioning, "Just WHAT was Sandra doing with Greg to get approvals?"

Sandra shared with me, "I feel like I'm being set up again. Greg deliberately put me in charge of this project knowing that it would continue to drive a wedge between me and the other women leaders. I know he has no intention of this working out. He just needs to show the board he's looked at it."

As Sandra continued to vent her frustrations, I listened carefully and said, "There could be another story that's just as true as the one you're telling yourself right now."

Sandra tossed that thought around in her head for an extra moment and finally said, "I don't or can't see what else could be going on."

I gently reminded Sandra that her current perspective wasn't the only one in play. "This really is a good opportunity for you and your female peers. Greg is in a tough place. The board needs to see something that shows the organization is being run well. That's what good boards do. They put pressure on the CEO and his/her team to prove they are taking care of today but also looking to the future. He could have led this himself, but since Greg can't do everything himself, he chose you. For three years now, who's been talking about innovation and continuous improvement?"

I continued in a supportive tone, "Sandra, remember we all are like heat-seeking missiles aimed at getting exactly what we want most. We all are addicted to being right, even you. Why does this continuous story of Greg being the bad guy fit for you? What if he's just like you? Trying to…"

Sandra blurted out, "Denise, all he cares about is money and looking good. He's controlling and sexist. He doesn't care about the employees' well-being nor really serving our customers! He undermines the Ops VP and won't give her, or the HR director, the guidance and resources they need to perform well. He's an awful leader."

"Maybe," I said "But you and I have talked about the research on leadership. Management performance is representative of the same bell curve as you see in anything else. What that means is most leaders are really average. Think about it. With any performance curve, at least 50 percent are considered average or below. But even if you look at the average, some are slightly above and below average. Those tending towards slightly below average are still performing well enough. Those who are performing better feel the drag of those performing slightly below average, and every one of those managers is doing the best they can."

I knew that even though they had this conversation numerous times over the last three years, it didn't matter. Sandra was learning to be a good leader, and in the scheme of things, this new assignment was an opportunity to take her leadership to an advanced level. Sandra is a great individual contributor. She completed projects and that's why senior executives loved people like her. They can give her a project and rest assured it will get done. The problem for Sandra is that what gets rewarded is one's ability to convince others around you to embrace and execute on an idea. What gets rewarded is one's ability to take a group of people and turn them into a team.

What gets rewarded is your ability to negotiate for what you want. Sandra hadn't done that.

"I just don't see it. They will never work with me," Sandra said.

I countered, "Maybe not at first, but over time—"

Sandra finished my sentence saying, "I know, small steps over time achieves remarkable results."

For the first year, Sandra and I agreed the biggest challenge was two-fold:

- To introduce the female managers (Ops and HR) to designing and implementing a major change initiative as neither had ever had that experience before. During the first year, Sandra got Greg to pay a significant sum for the team to go through certification training using design thinking. It was a huge victory.
- To get the other two management women to show up and contribute in meetings on some level. Sandra began coaching the other female managers on how to manage up, how to approach Greg on a level that was comfortable to him so that he could see the advantages to what they were bringing forward.

At first, the women did not want to be coached. They did not see the value of collaboration. But Sandra continued to stay firm to her commitment to helping them develop as a team. Over time Sandra was able to see the women take on more and more responsibility for the work and to offer new ideas to Greg.

About eight months later, the HR Director developed the confidence to present new and progressive ideas. Greg approved all three recommendations. A HUGE win.

- The HR Director had completed a plan to elevate the salary discrepancy between men and women. That meant all three of the women on the senior team would be in the same salary range as the men on the team.

- Sandra and the HR Director asked for additional headcount based upon a thorough analysis of the work and how the additional headcount could improve operations.
- Sandra was able to hire someone to update and modernize the web experience for both employees and customers.

Two years later, the innovation leadership was stronger, and the women made progress getting small innovation projects completed. They learned to trust each other and work together to get their ideas approved in spite of Greg's habitual first answer of no.

LEADING CHANGE IS EXHAUSTING

Sandra learned techniques and specific skills on guiding change when you're not totally in charge of the people or resources. She learned how to manage up the ladder in a less disruptive way. She learned how to get people to change their minds, even her co-executives, slowly, over time.

The process was personally exhausting. It was a big chess game with a need to see a few moves ahead. Having me in her corner helped Sandra see four steps ahead so she would not get frustrated and just stop trying when the first attempt failed.

For each of us, deciding to lead a change initiative is more than adding or upgrading technology or changing part or all of the business operations. Sustained change requires us to think broadly and cultivate skills that threaten our current sense of security and self-worth.

REMARKABLE LEADERSHIP LESSONS

- **Core Skills:** The foundation for good effective leadership is based on our ability to see an outcome, gather resources, delegate tasks, follow up, and ensure follow-through. The rub for most people is failing to learn how to do one or more of these core skills or how to adapt them to the circumstances at hand. Managing the tension that comes with change is an art that can only be learned through deliberate practice.

- **Identifying the Source of Resistance:** Resistance or indifference to change generally is tied to how the person feels about their chances of doing a good job. Too often the real reasons for resisting change are hidden by expansive explanations on why something won't work or is too risky. To achieve success, you must first determine whether resistance is due to a lack of will to make an effort, or a fear of failure because they don't believe they have the skill to do well. Then you can make a plan to overcome the resistance.

- **Open to a Different Point of View:** Resistance and procrastination are outcomes derived from our beliefs—our need to be successful and safe. As executives and leaders, our busy, *got-to-get-it-done* lives, blind us to even entertaining that there's another viewpoint. Being able to listen to and embrace another point of view (even when that point of view isn't the same as yours), and make others feel like you hear them, have considered their point of view, and can provide them with a way to seize the opportunity—unleashes the potential in all of us.

SECTION IV
LEADERSHIP TRAINING
AND ORGANIZATIONAL
DEVELOPMENT

IDEAS  ACTION

PERFORMANCE IS RELATIVE

DENISEism:
We look to those around us and decide
what level is worth our efforts.

"We take better care of our smartphones
than we do ourselves!"

Arianna Huffington

MINIMIZE BARRIERS

Director: Good morning! Glad to see you. How'd you like
                 getting all those emails this weekend?

New employee: Well to be honest… they confused me. They made
                 me feel like I'd forgotten something, and I really
                 try to be thorough in completing my work. They
                 ended up making me feel like I wasn't doing a
                 good job.

Director: Oh… I sent them to give you my ideas. It's my way
                 of getting things off my mind.

New employee: I didn't know what you wanted me to do with them, especially since most of them were covered in the work I'd already given you. I spent a great deal of time on what I gave you, and my goal was to make sure you had everything you needed when you needed it. That way my time off is for me to rejuvenate.

Colleague: (Overhearing the exchange, later told the new employee) I heard what the Director told you. You'll get used to her just sending you emails on the weekend and after hours. They're her brain farts, and she just sends them out as they come to her.

New employee: But what am I to do with them? Besides, as a manager, I'd never send out text messages during off hours that weren't an emergency. Otherwise when do we get down time?

Colleague: Don't worry about them. If you've covered the basics, then the rest of it doesn't matter. The Director rarely comes back to them.

New employee: How do you know what's really important and what's not?

Colleague: Well... you just learn over time. Don't worry; you're doing well. She really likes you.

This is a real conversation. Some of you may recognize this conversation because you've experienced some portion of it. I'm sure the Director is trying to be helpful. In fact, if you read about a lot of CEOs, they talk about sending emails and text messages to their staff at all hours of the day, night, and weekends.

In 2014, 42 percent of working Americans surveyed said they didn't take ANY vacation. Too many say they don't take vacation because they are always "on." With our ability to IM, text, and email at all hours, there's an expectation that when you get the message from your boss, you're to respond. Yet, we know that everyone needs down time.

The myth of the successful executive burning the candle at both ends is just that. Arianna Huffington's book *Thrive*, details from a very personal point of view how her choices to live up to that myth nearly killed her. Now she is on a mission to educate others on the effects of sleep deprivation and no time off.

I love her comments that we take better care of our smartphones than we do of ourselves. We all know you have to turn off and recharge your smartphone, so why do we think our bodies don't deserve the same?

As the HR manager at a plant, I remember having to set standards for overtime so that we achieved a balance between production needs and making sure our employees were alert and able to work safely. There were employees who would take any and every shift available. A lack of sleep causes people to make poor decisions and slows their reaction time down. In a manufacturing plant, that can be a deadly combination.

The second issue with the Director's actions relates to the latest focus on employee engagement. For over thirty years, we've known up to 15 percent of a company's entire workforce (management to front line) is highly engaged. The rest are somewhere between moderately to fully disengaged. Let me translate… engagement is a code word for productivity.

So, if 80 percent of your management team is disengaged and is doing things to cause their staff to be moderately to fully disengaged, what's that doing to your bottom line and competitive edge in the marketplace?

Managers who are unable or unwilling to allow their staff to take some recuperative down time are contributing to an erosion of your company's profitability.

Whether you're the Director or a new employee, it is important to have the conversation about priority setting. If you don't, you're doing a disservice to yourself and your company. It's the first step to higher productivity.

REMARKABLE LEADERSHIP LESSONS

- **Priority Setting:** Concern about our relationships gets in the way of setting priorities. For an employee, the fear is about how a boss will evaluate him/her in the future "if I say no," when the "do more with less" directive mandates that somehow it is possible to do everything without sacrificing anything. For managers, these messages impede transparency and make it tough to know the organization's capacity limits until things break down.

- **Resource Management:** Today, we have so many ways to access more resources to find solutions. As a manager, make sure you are thinking about the full range of talent that can be brought to bear towards solving a problem. The range includes using contract workers, gig workers, vendors, or partners to create a short-term developmental opportunity for others inside or outside your department.

- **The New Boss:** The toughest time for employees is when a new supervisor is hired. Often a new supervisor, while learning the ropes, resorts to assigning busy work to be seen as "jumping right in." A manager, searching for ways to feel relevant and prove worth, might try to change existing work processes or systems to immediately "improve" things. Aligning values to what's important toward getting the mission accomplished helps with transitions.

    We know that everyone feels uncomfortable when put in the position of disagreeing with the behavior of their new manager. In your organization, what ways do you message when/ if disagreement is appropriate? How does a new member of the management team learn to accept—and value—differing opinions and measure the impact and level of transparency in your organization?

Monitoring the ways people feel comfortable to speak up, where transparency is inappropriate, and embedding conversational skills in both formal and informal training is key to minimizing barriers to higher performance.

PROFILE: SOOTHING THE TASMANIAN DEVIL

DENISEism:
Admitting that you're not going to be great at
every leadership skill is the sign of a smart leader.

Not everything is for everyone. If developing others isn't your strength, then hire someone to do it for you. If implementing an idea isn't your strength, then surround yourself with those who love implementing strategies and then get out of the way.

The Board of a midsized technology company called me to discuss the new CEO they'd hired. They loved his experience, high energy, and creativity, but they feared that he was causing havoc with some top performing team members. They had two managers in particular the Board worried about losing.

After meeting with Kevin, the CEO, I felt like I had been through a blender. He talked so fast, dropping various ideas, thoughts, and visions as if he was adding ingredients for a smoothie! How was anyone supposed to understand which idea he truly wanted to develop or how to get there?

Kevin would have benefitted from some coaching for himself but was not open to it. He told me that he didn't want to fire two of his leading people, but felt he wasn't getting the best from them. From his point of view, he passed on all his new ideas and suggestions, and Suzanne and Doug weren't taking the bull by the horns and running with any of it. What Kevin was actually doing was running his meetings and directing his managers like the Tasmanian Devil cartoon character. He'd rush in, drop a load of options and ideas, and leave the room with his stunned, immobile team recovering and wondering what to do next.

Kevin was very clear that what he needed was someone who could run a risk analysis on his ideas and help him think through the options and cost of changes. Kevin expected his Executive Vice Presidents to figure out how to restructure the departments to meet the competitive challenges the company was facing. He asked me to please talk with Suzanne and Doug.

I realized that if Kevin was not open to coaching, I could work with the at-risk managers to coach them on how to get what they needed from Kevin so they could do the job Kevin expected of them.

Doug was not evolving with the new challenges the company was facing. Doug, unfortunately, was not open to coaching and was very closed to making any changes to the way he carried out his responsibilities for fear that it would result in losing "power." When I told Doug that one of the women on his team was undermining him deliberately, he wouldn't hear anything about it. He could not make the changes necessary to move his department to success. Doug was eventually fired due to poor leadership skills. The woman I warned him about was promoted to take his place, and then she was eventually fired as well.

I worked successfully with Suzanne (a quiet, introverted finance person), to help her find her voice to share her thoughts on what would and wouldn't work. Awarded and recognized in the past for excellent practices, Suzanne was getting lost when the market, technology, and landscape of the business climate was changing. Her strength was implementation. As an implementer, she needed time to play with a new model, touch and feel it. Envision how it would play out in various scenarios. Compare it to the old style.

I taught Suzanne how to envision what the new business model looked like, how to talk through the business model with her staff, and then how to take an idea from her supervisors and implement it, as well as, how to present her team's ideas to her supervisor and get him to sign off. Essentially, I coached Suzanne on how to manage up by helping her teach Kevin about the new model and how it was different, resulting in new systems and processes that needed to be put into place, which would change the way things were done.

Suzanne learned how to engage Kevin so she knew what he wanted and could sort through which ideas were workable and which were pie in the sky. She learned how to quickly and succinctly show Kevin the impact of the change on the business model, reactions from customers and referral partners, as well as holding Kevin and her staff accountable for making decisions and then following-through on plans.

REMARKABLE LEADERSHIP TOOL:
BUSINESS MODEL CANVAS

The Business Model Canvas is a tool to compare and contrast the old business model with the new. Suzanne was able to envision and imagine a new model based on what needed to change: What, when, and the order in which things needed to change. Cost and revenue projections to make better decisions were brought to the front to enable Suzanne to communicate with Kevin about next steps to bring to the Board.

What she found out by going through the process was that she was able to ask better questions of Kevin, slow him down, get better control on the systems, communicate the systems, and plan more easily/clearly. And, simultaneously, she was able to communicate more clearly with her staff and peers on how to align financial obligations, new costs, shifting costs, and jobs with which they weren't familiar.

REMARKABLE LEADERSHIP TOOL: DEFINING CULTURE

Culture is the super-power that drives implementation. It's a lot easier to think all you have to do is hire the right talent, put them in a room, and somehow a conversation about culture turns into something meaningful. It doesn't. Culture is how things get done every day. It defines acceptable behaviors within your organization. We can define the culture of any organization by paying attention to what is discussed (or not discussed), rewarded, and recognized. It takes as much planning and work to shape your organization's culture as it does to decide what products and services to offer and to whom.

Culture is the operating system for every business. This operating system translates every idea on how your business will run into behaviors, boundaries, and expectations for how everyone works together. Culture determines how costs will be incurred, how decisions are made, how ethics and integrity are defined, and more importantly, it's the framework defining your reputation.

Diagnose the culture—You understand the culture by asking questions and listening to the stories shared between employees and how employees informally enculturate new hires.

- How does someone get fired around here?
- Are decisions made before the meeting and announced in the meeting, in the meeting, or after the meeting?
- Which decisions are implemented?
- If you're traveling, do you stay at a Holiday Inn (budget-conscious motel), or the Wynn Resorts (high-end hotel)?

- What is our negotiation strategy with our vendors? Are they partners for the long haul or an expense to be minimized?
- If you are a customer, how are you treated when your expectations are missed? Who and how many people are required to sign off on an exception?
- Who are the people who quietly get things done because they are the experts at getting it done?
- What are the ethical dilemmas faced and how are they addressed?
- How does a project die?

Great ideas are nothing without the ability to implement them. Conversations are more than just exchanging ideas. It's the stories we tell and how they've changed in our head after the discussion. The best conversations make us uncomfortable, and then cause us to want to change our behavior to relieve that discomfort.

REMARKABLE LEADERSHIP LESSONS

- **Create a shared understanding.** When asked to restate what they heard, can your team members do so correctly in their own words?
- **Create shared meaning.** Can others talk on the same level about implications and consequences and identify risks and opportunities?
- **Create shared expectations.** Do others understand what the result will be when whatever it is that is being asked of them is done? Brené Brown calls it, "knowing what done looks like." It's not just achieving the result that counts, but also that how the result was achieved has to be the same in everyone's mind.

THE IMPACT OF VIRTUOUS AND VICIOUS CYCLES IN MEETINGS

DENISEism:
Surviving the Shark Frenzy.

One January, I attended a networking meeting where the facilitator asked each of us to write down our goals for the year. Additionally, we were asked to fast forward to the end of the year and tell the group our proudest moment.

As we went around the room, you heard all the typical goals: lose weight, double my sales, exercise, kids graduating from college, publish a book, get a job, start a business. But there was one person, Maxwell, who said he was struggling. He posed, "If we all believe in an infinitely intelligent and loving Creator, how can we believe that it would create anything that is unlike itself?" Maxwell went on to say that he would like to reach the end of December and say "I heard and followed the life plan that the Creator had in store for me. I tamed my fears, found the courage, and lived and acted out of faith."

The silence was palpable.

I thought, *what can you say to that? He's either the bravest person I've met or the craziest!* Either way Maxwell struck a chord, and not just with me. What followed was a series of questions about how he was going to make money doing this. How would he know he was following the path laid out by the Creator? Did the Creator speak to him, and how would he know it's the Creator speaking versus just his own desire?

That's when it hit me. I've seen this kind of intense questioning before. In my work with executives, I have observed that anyone who brings a new or innovative idea to the table often endures the same kind of intense scrutiny.

If an idea is something familiar, then the questioning from others at the table is positive and supportive. But if the idea is something new, the questioning will feel like you're in a shark frenzy. People in the room will ask questions and make statements in rapid fire succession. The tone hints (and sometimes not so subtly) that the presenter is daft.

I can assure you that at nearly every meeting you attend, regardless of the level of the people in the room, someone is sitting on the sideline with an idea on how to do something better, faster, easier… but not saying anything because they fear the, "shark frenzy" effect.

Maxwell had a shark frenzy on his hands. His response? He was silent and took in everyone's questions. Then he responded by saying, "Thank you for all the love, care, and concern you've expressed. I've thought about this path for a while." He continued, "There are no guarantees in life. But I feel that if I say I believe in an infinitely good, wise, all-knowing, and loving Creator, then I can't believe that I would design a better plan than His. For once in my life, I'm going to have a Life Plan, not a business plan. I will continue to work my business, but I will allow for and be open to the possibility that there is a better plan in store for me. My message to you is, I ask that you do the same."

The air in the room was so thick you could cut it with a knife. The meetings after the meeting continued the shark frenzy. Maxwell's Don Quixote view of life continued at every meeting. Each time I saw Maxwell, I wondered if and what he was hearing from the Creator. Did he tame his fears? Had he found the courage to follow the path laid out for him? Most importantly, I wanted to know if he was happy.

REMARKABLE LEADERSHIP LESSONS

- **Don't Shoot the Messenger.** As a leader there are times when you have to take a tough stand for values that your people are not going to understand. Most likely it's because it's pushing them so far out of their comfort zone, they will seriously resist. How you respond in those moments sends a message throughout the organization.

- **Reacting to the Hard Truth.** Is your team able to tell you the hard truth and know you'll be okay with it? Are you able to tell them the hard truth in a way that lets them know they were heard and that you believe in their ability to find the right answer?

- **Finding the Way.** As a leader you don't always see the "how" to find the way to get something to the finish line. Someone else could find the way, if you're bold enough to ask for help and humble enough to listen to suggestions. If you restrain from "here's why that won't work" instant rejection, you will encourage the more reticent to offer their input. It might be you (the leader), or it might be the messenger who has the winning solution.

A LEADER'S BEST PROBLEM SOLVING SKILL: COLLABORATIVE THINKING

Einstein said, "You can't solve a problem by using the same kind of thinking we used to create the problem."

You've got a problem? No. You've got a really BIG problem. What do you do? Me, I would call a few friends and ask their opinion. I wouldn't call just anyone. I'd call people who I thought could help me solve the problem. I'd describe the situation and ask for their advice.

I don't know about your friends, but mine would give me their best advice, and from their collective wisdom, I'd figure out what's what and get to work. So, is this a reasonable way to solve a problem?

For a couple of years now, I've been speaking to HR professionals on how to get the best solutions to the really big problems facing their companies. HR geeks call this Talent Management. To the rest of the world, it's recognized as being mentored.

At a presentation to a group of HR professionals, I asked if they knew about Crowdsourcing. Crowdsourcing is the act of taking a job traditionally performed by a designated agent (usually an employee) and outsourcing it to an undefined, generally large group of people in the form of an open call. The blank stares that looked back at me were a bit unnerving, folks. Here was a room full of HR professionals—people tasked with helping their company figure out how to best harness minds to solve problems—and they knew nothing about this idea.

To explain how crowdsourcing might help with BIG problem-solving, I shared a story I heard in the news. James Cameron, Director of the movies, *The Abyss* and *Titantic*, heard about BP's major oil spill and decided to jump in to help solve BP's problem. Cameron called BP, and I imagine the conversation went something like this:

> Cameron: "Hey, I'm a pretty intelligent guy with a lot of experience in deep water exploration. I've got equipment, some pretty smart friends who know something about drilling, and I'd like to help you figure this out."
>
> BP dismissed him with, "We've got it covered. Thanks, but no thanks."

Cameron did what many of us in corporate America do when the boss tells you they've got it covered. He believed them. As time went on, Cameron watched in dismay as he realized—"Hmmm, BP doesn't have a clue how to plug the oil spill or clean up the resulting mess."

James Cameron is a director, a producer. He didn't take this lying down as his love for the ocean and environment is radically intense. A man of action (he literally shouts "action" all day at people!), he held a ten-hour brainstorming session with his friends, their friends, and some folks from government agencies, including the EPA, to try to come up with a few ideas (without BP's input).

Can you imagine all these really smart, talented, concerned, self-motivated people in a room working on the problem of the century? I wish I had been there. This is the work I so love to do and the kind of people with whom I love to do it. Imagine it! That room was filled with the best and most creative minds, all focused on answering three questions: How to stop the leak, how to clean up the environment, and how to prevent it from happening again.

When an executive intentionally is looking for solutions to a big problem, s/he may formally set up a meeting and bring in outside experts to solve the big, thorny issues, but the idea of crowdsourcing is really just a new name on an old practice. Brainstorming, networking, mastermind meetings, even study groups you may be assigned to if you attend an executive leadership program, are gatherings to bring different perspectives, knowledge, skills, expertise, and wisdom into a shared conversation.

Crowdsourcing is often free and can jumpstart a stagnating team into creating alternate solutions to a problem that has plagued a department or company. Sometimes you can use focus groups of users/clients/customers. Sometimes you can put the question on the web and ask for feedback.

Netflix did just that. They offered a $1,000,000 prize for the person or team that could come up with an algorithm that could increase the accuracy of their recommendation engine and thus better predict DVD rentals. Unfortunately, by the time the solution was useable, Netflix had new problems. Streaming was taking off and DVD rentals were declining fast. The upside was that although they didn't use the information as intended, it moved them further along on the idea that big data could predict consumer viewing preferences. That's the downside of big, bold initiatives; they take time, and in a fast-moving environment, the final conclusions could be irrelevant.

My goal for the presentation was to help these HR professionals understand and hopefully begin to measure the impact of initiatives on engagement and productivity. In many parts of an organization, managers and employees spend as much as 50 percent of their time in meetings. It's the kind of thing we joke about but don't look to see if it's all worth it. As it is, too many are overwhelmed and suffer from decision fatigue because of all the other time- and energy-sucking activities (responding to emails, instant messaging, and hallway conversations to stay in the know) which they feel they have to do just to stay ahead of the curve.

All this busy activity is eroding productivity. It makes people *feel* productive, but the data isn't pointing to better results. What does it take to change your mind? That's a huge question for HR practitioners. How do you get people—especially managers—to stop doing things that may be counterproductive?

REMARKABLE LEADERSHIP TOOL: SOCIAL NETWORK ANALYSIS

Using big data on the social connections in an organization is a relatively new development in the field of HR. Information can bring prestige, power, and/or personal reward. Early reports indicate that all that activity is costing each of us. About 5 percent of employees generate 20–30 percent of the value of collaboration. Internal crowdsourcing and networks such as employee resource groups can improve productivity.

REMARKABLE LEADERSHIP LESSONS

However you choose to do it, step away from preconceived ideas, the same old routine, and existing protocol to work on new solutions to a challenge or problem or vision. Whether it's crowdsourcing, going on a retreat, setting up challenges or contests among employees or customers/clients, bringing in an outsider to facilitate discussions, or anything else that gets minds working on alternate concepts, you can't keep doing the same thing and expect different results. Make a radical change to grow something new!

Turn Listening into Action

I coach my clients to use the information they gather in listening sessions to move into action and achieve results.

- Gather the repeated complaints or reasons people are frustrated.
- Then have a meeting to talk about them. Instead of asking for solutions, ask open-ended questions to find out why they continue to do things that most likely impede productivity and cause more work. Good questions start the attendees thinking about possibilities.
  - What if we could…?
  - What would it be like if…?
  - If you had a magic wand and could start all over again… what would be different?

Once the possibilities are out, ask open-ended questions that bring out reservations.

- Talk about first steps.
  - What is one small step we could take to change this situation?
  - How would we know we are making progress?
  - What would others outside this room, this conversation, need to hear to make a small change that would move us closer to what we envisioned earlier?

Oh, in case you're wondering what happened with Cameron and BP? I've researched and reached out to a number of people to learn the conclusion of this story. Found nothing. Then I got to thinking about it. How many initiatives are started with major fanfare and lots of activity only to fizzle out in a few months, with no word shared as to what happened nor why it suddenly fell off the radar? And we wonder why getting employees to pay attention and change behavior is so hard. To change, we have to believe it's not only worth it but that it will actually happen.

CATCH ME IF YOU CAN

DENISEism:
What we say in public and
what we do are not always aligned.

Diversity is a strength (or that's what people say in public). However, what we do in practice is a different thing. Implementing true diversity practices and equal opportunity programs is hard, and although I can make a business case on how it impacts the viability of ANY business, I don't think the vast majority of senior executives truly care a wit about it.

You may protest, saying, "That can't be true." Or you may think that as a Black woman, of course I would have that opinion. Maybe. But I have worked with executives who have told me flat out (when I brought up the illegality of discrimination): "I haven't been caught yet. If we are [caught] it's just the cost of doing business".

Don't take my word alone. I asked a colleague who is white, male, and has over thirty years as a Human Resources professional. My colleague shared with me his experiences.

> *I've not been successful in my career convincing my employ-*
> *ers there is a business case for diversity. I imagine if my*
> *employers had been consumer products companies, where*

those companies want to reflect the values of all their customers, this would have been different. I've only worked for intermediate suppliers—manufacturing companies that were selling some component to be sent to another company and used to build a final product. My last two employers were less than $500M in sales, and companies that size just don't have the resources nor the mindset to see value in diversity sensitivity. Furthermore, some of them are willing to quietly violate affirmative action and EEO laws too.

One government contractor refused to develop an affirmative action plan for over forty years. I handled the OFCCP audit when they finally got caught. The outcome was no more than a conciliation agreement (a written warning) that said they will remain in compliance from this point forward. Fines were minimal. Nobody went to jail. None of their contracts were lost. To them, it was worth the risk.

On another occasion I was the Director Organizational Development for a $1.5B company, that had acquired businesses doing the same thing with compliance. I took on this issue and defended it all the way to the Board level. The Board supported HR's position on this matter, but can you imagine the grief and resistance I faced with the leaders of the acquired business? Not just in EEO2/AAP3 compliance, but recruiting, succession planning, leadership development, and every area of OD. There's a lot to be said for those HR people who are administrative, do as they're told, and don't rock the boat. You can work many years for one company and retire having done very little.

---

[2] EEO= Equal Employment Opportunity
[3] AAP= Affirmative Action Program/Plan

Looking at the numbers, in 2019:

- American corporations earned about $2.13 Trillion in 2019.
- OFCCP[4] filed 55 conciliatory agreements, totaling about $40M in fines
- EEOC[5] filed 73K charges for a total of $505M penalties.

Given how few OFCCP inspections result in any kind of financial penalty and how few EEOC cases are filed, many executives just say, "Why bother? Catch me if you can."

After reading this I hope you are not disheartened. I included this section to help us all understand the nature and challenge of change. The popular wisdom is such that if the leader says to do it a certain way and then puts a policy in place, everyone will follow. Every organization and workplace has visible and invisible behaviors that are acceptable and unacceptable. Figuring out the nuances of going beyond diversity (which means we ask people who are different from us to be a part of our social circle) means that senior executives have to understand what inclusion and belonging means in their organization in real time. Then, understand what it means when everything shifts, and they have to manage the dangers inherent in change. It brings different opinions, ways of doing, seeing, thinking, and being, into play.

For a list of conciliatory agreements go to the Freedom of Information website: https://www.dol.gov/agencies/ofccp/foia/library

---

[4] OFCCP = Office of Federal Contract Compliance Programs
[5] EEOC = Equal Employment Opportunity Commission

INCLUSION AND BELONGING

It's true that organizations need to remain aware of the negative impact on and legal consequences to businesses from issues and disparities in education, wealth generation, health care, and mental health. Savvy executives skilled at the process of leading, know that just recognizing that there could be a problem doesn't change hearts, minds, and behavior.

There are valid issues to be addressed and (as with any change) you can't make sustainable progress by ignoring the perspectives of everyone. That's why making headway on inclusion and belonging is dependent on our ability to hold conversations around collaboration. We have to learn, practice, reflect, and then try again and again to listen better—without being triggered.

To gain insights from your team and create a collaborative environment, you have to understand where they are coming from, and what they bring with them. To allow them to share openly, you have to take ownership of your response. What is your intention in each conversation? And what lens do you look through, listen with, when someone is speaking and sharing?

- A key value to hold is that everyone in the room is smart, caring, and invested in being successful.
- We have to practice forgiveness when people don't live up to our expectations.

- We must hold others and ourselves to a standard of taking ownership for decisions.
- A conversation without action leads to disappointment.
- If you're going to ask, you have to do something about it.

To make Inclusion and Belonging work, everyone has to be committed to mastering relationship skills. Focus on three things: Ownership, Intention, and the Lens and Filters used to form your perspectives.

Ownership

Ownership means being responsible for work and the impact of our behavior, not just our intention. What I mean is that we have to remember that intention is invisible, and we are judged by the impact of our actions.

Ownership involves self-determination or agency: being committed to managing trust, optimism, resilience, and our credibility with others; choosing to demonstrate a positive reaction when receiving feedback. My mother would say, "If you're grown enough to ask, then be grown enough to hear what I have to say." Over time, I realized she meant you determine when and how to react. You choose to be angry when others say, do, or think something different from you. You choose how to respond, to stay or go. Each has consequences and change doesn't happen in an instant.

Intention

We always engage others from our intention, but people always judge us by the impact of our behavior. Intention is invisible. I cannot see your intention. I can ASSUME it. But I can only trust you and know you by your works.

Lenses and Filters

We can only see the world, and process our interactions, through the lenses that we look through—which are different for each of us. If we grow up with abusive parents or neighbors, we live in a war zone, are ignored by our parents, or we find ourselves rejected because of our religion, sexual preference, amount of money we have, are ridiculed for the way we dress, the color of our skin or hair, the language we speak or accent we have; we see the world through those lenses.

One thing I know is that people NOT in the majority tend to observe very well. When we see people in the news or in authority treat each other poorly or with prejudice, and everybody acts like "it's no big deal," we know that as bad as that is, it's ten times worse for people in the minority. People in power will legitimize their behavior and opinions/beliefs as being correct through the laws that are passed, the code of ethics followed, and behaviors become more and more blatant.

Creating inclusive workplaces where EVERYONE understands their role, what they have to learn, how they need to embrace and change their behavior and perspective is tough. It's not impossible, but the past 100+ years have taught us that what we focus on is what we get, and the more we focus on the parts, the less likely we are to change the whole system.

REMARKABLE LEADERSHIP LESSONS

- **Who Benefits?** Before you can change anything, you have to see how everyone is benefiting from the current system. Every organization is made up of processes that connect, foster, and fuel its current results. Anyone who tries to point out what is wrong or should be changed is on dangerous ground.

- **Cultural change can only be dealt with by changing values, beliefs, habits, and loyalties.** You cannot tell someone how to be inclusive and open to diversity and not address all the other ways people get rewarded and punished for their behaviors.
- **Destabilize Status Quo.** For any organizational change to happen, you need to destabilize the status quo. Executives are usually not paid for and do not acquire power by destabilizing the status quo, especially if the status quo is achieving results.
- **There are no shortcuts to changing a culture.** It takes strategic diagnosis, planning, and implementation over at least an eight-year period. From the first day, an organization has a formed structure, culture, and automatic responses are developed. We learn how to be with each other by how we treat each other, how we hold each other accountable/responsible, and how we allow the decision makers to control how we treat each other.

REMARKABLE LEADERSHIP EDGE: CONVERSATIONS THAT DEFINE THE STRUCTURE OF YOUR CULTURE

Questions to ask if you want to diagnose your organization's Diversity, Inclusion, and Belonging practices.

- What happens when someone yells, is in heated debate, takes long lunches, misses deadlines?
- Who socializes with whom? When? Where?
- What jokes are acceptable, tolerated, and spread throughout the organization?
- What happens when someone tells the unspoken truth?
- How does your HR department promote, protect, reward, and defend management?
- Name the instances when HR successfully promotes, protects, rewards and defends non-management employees?
- Who and how are troublemakers, disrupters, and those with different ideas treated when they step outside the norm?

- What happens when someone (particularly an executive), doesn't have all the answers or is incompetent?
- As a change agent, on a scale of 1–10 (where 1 is can't/won't engage in conflict, 5 is dancing around the edges of disruption, and 10 is skilled at managing conflict,—knowing when to turn up the heat and how to let everyone cool off and still move forward) where do you see yourself? What is one thing you can do to move one step closer to a 10?
- How do you know who is a high performer, smart person, or rising star? Ask people who are the high performers, smart people, or rising stars in your organization. What do they do? Then ask the same question for those who are not.

Ask these questions to as many people as you can. Don't judge, evaluate, or try and explain the answers. Just listen.

Once you have them all collected, look for the patterns (positive and negative). Did they change your thinking?

BROKEN HEART SYNDROME

DENISEism:
The tragic mistake of leaving
our personal problems at the door.

One of my podcast guests was Carla Carlisle. At the time of our interview, Carla was an IT executive at a Fortune 500 company in Charlotte, NC., and she had just written her book called *Journey to the Son*. My podcast, *Closing the Gap with Denise Cooper*, features ordinary people who share the lessons learned as they lead change at work or within the community.

Carla shared a story of a coworker who was having a hard time in his personal life. He and his wife were going through a messy divorce and were in the midst of a custody battle over their son. As time went on, this man had become withdrawn but was still a good performer. When asked if he was all right, he responded, "I'm fine, nothing to worry about." As I heard the story, I imagined how many people asked him if he was okay and got the same response even though, they knew he couldn't be fine when he was going through such a traumatic time in his life.

What Carla didn't know was that her coworker hadn't seen his child in months, and it was tearing him up on the inside. At office meetings, he was in control, had been in his job for years, and was still quite capable of performing well, but there was something amiss. It wasn't until several months later that she connected the dots. By then it was too late.

One day a colleague ran into Carla's office to ask if she saw the news. She replied, "What news?" With frantic motions, the colleague ushered Carla to the computer monitor. As they hurried out of her office, there on the monitor was breaking news... The announcer said that Carla's coworker had taken his son to the top floor of a high rise and first thrown his son off the side of the building and then jumped. Both plunged to their deaths. In the most horrible way possible, the whole team found out just how much stress their coworker had been hiding from them all along.

This well-performing employee had repeatedly turned away support from his coworkers, while internally, he denied his heart was breaking until he could not take it anymore. I can only imagine how the thought of losing his only son began to slowly, over time, consume him, until only his fear of losing his son forever dominated his every thought.

When you're not telling the truth, I, as a coworker/employer, can feel that you are not fully present, and that puts up a block between us. Carla felt something was wrong with her coworker, as did others in the office. Both sides have to find the courage to ask about that feeling that something is off, and both sides have to be willing to listen without judgement to the answers.

How would things have changed if Carla's coworker could have shared his pain about not seeing his child for months, or his fear of losing the right to see his child? What would have been different if he had shared and Carla and her peers could have found a way to help him live with divorce? Would he and/or his child be alive today? How would it have changed Carla? How might it have given license for men to talk about their pain at work? The system can't just automatically change and welcome your personhood; you have to be true to yourself.

BROKEN HEART SYNDROME IS PHYSICAL AND REAL

Carla's coworker was in pain from his heart breaking over losing his son. Our bodies are not designed to be in fear for long periods of time. Significant bodies of research on the heart-brain connection, our connection to other humans and animals, stress, sleep, and weight gain, show clear patterns of the damage living in fear does to our body, mind, and spirit. The longer we are fearful and distrustful, the less we are able to find our way out.

Functional magnetic resonance imaging, (fMRI) looks at blood flow in the brain to detect areas of activity. fMRIs show graphically how our thinking narrows to the point of shutting down our cognitive ability when in the midst of a challenge or fear, until all we see is the problem, and our energy is focused on how to solve it or relieve the pain immediately.

Thus, when faced with overwhelming anxiety either in business or personal life, our ability to think rationally becomes nearly nonexistent. The limbic system that determines emotion and carries emotional memories is mixed into the chemical cocktail that regulates our normal intuitive or gut reactions. The prefrontal cortex, which governs logic, reasoning, and critical thinking diminishes.

In real time, you will focus all your questions and answers in pursuit of, "Why is this happening? What does it mean? What if (fill in the worst-case scenarios)?" Because we can't see a way to live with the worst case, we then feel trapped and helpless. Fear has won.

Continuously thinking about the "problem" creates a chemical cocktail that, over the long-term, takes its toll on our bodies in the form of anxiety and stress.

It bears saying that stress itself is not an illness; rather, it is a state of being. With that said, it is a very powerful cause of illness.

Long-term excessive stress is known to lead to serious health problems. Numerous medical studies indicate stress worsens or increases the risk of conditions like obesity, heart disease, Alzheimer's disease, diabetes, depression, infertility, gastrointestinal problems, migraines, panic attacks, a compromised immune system, and asthma. Not to mention the increase in avoidance behaviors of alcoholism, drug use, sex addiction, overeating/bulimia, exercise addiction, cutting, etc. to counteract the stress momentarily.

*The way we do anything
is the way we do everything.*

Martha Beck

*Motivation is what gets you started.
Habit is what keeps you going.*

Jim Ryun

We all perform at our best when under the right amount of pressure. Derek Rogers, PhD, and Nick Petrie, in their book, *Work Without Stress*, explain the distinction between good stress and bad stress. Their book calls for greater understanding of the difference between the pressure to perform (good stress) and rumination (bad stress).

They refer to short-term stress, which motivates us to take action, as acute stress. This is often known as pressure to perform. Continuously thinking about and replaying what happened in the past or potential consequences in the future, is referred to as rumination. Long-term rumination without action leads to excessive or chronic stress.

Over time the impact of chronic stress becomes too much and our performance suffers not just at work, but in all areas of our lives. For all of us, continuously working under excessive or chronic stress starts to appear normal. We develop behavioral habits and counter-measures to deal with our situations.

SOCIAL ISOLATION PAIN

We know now, from science, that social isolation actually creates pain in the body; physical pain that causes the immune system to break down. Dr. Andrea Molberg, an organizational psychologist, shared with me on my podcast, *Closing the Gap with Denise Cooper*, that "We like people based on character first, but we like groups not based on a person's character but based on similarities, because it makes us feel safe."

When you're the only *one*, feeling different creates a sense of doubt. Social isolation is the feeling of not being connected to the group, team, or tribe. Long ago it was dangerous to be isolated, we were and still are safer in groups. The need to fit in is compelling not just from a psychological point of view, but our biological make-up drives us to connect with others.

Imagine being at work or school as a person of color, a woman, a person who prefers a partner of the same sex, or attending a religious service different than your own. You look around and see you are the only one like you, and everyone looks at you and wonders, *why are you here? How did you get an invitation?* And, even after being introduced and welcomed by a member, the sometimes subtle (and often not so subtle) questions or comments are asked about whether you belong there or not.

The longer you are in the group, the more you want to be a part of the group. For people of color and women, there are moments when you question whether you've gone too far and lost yourself. That feeling of being lost is exacerbated when you go home.

At home you've got to code switch back into this other person to get along with the people in your home and community. And maybe you code switch again when you go out to a nightclub or social event with your closest friends, or people in your house of worship, or volunteer at a nonprofit you believe in. So, you're always asking "Which person am I?" It becomes an identity crisis of sorts which becomes isolating.

It's easier to just be by yourself than to always be "On," trying to be what others want you to be. At some point you have say, "Where am I going to draw the line? How am I going to draw the line? What does that mean to me in drawing that line?"

In my experience as a woman of color, when I am working with people in the majority, I come with the knowledge that, you're not going to be comfortable in my world. But those in the majority have an expectation that I'm going to be comfortable in theirs. And mostly, that isn't the reality.

Imagine someone working all day and going home to an empty home. All day long believing he may never see his son again, and knowing his ex-wife doesn't want to be with him anymore. As well as, thinking about the life and dreams that were dashed, and wondering, perhaps, if he had any worth in the world any longer. Social isolation, combined with a lack of empathy or compassion from people, who didn't know his problems, because he couldn't share and unburden, led to tragic behaviors as an "only" solution. Can we in business be more available or provide some resources for our fellow humans?

REMARKABLE LEADERSHIP LESSONS

As an HR executive, I had an open door policy. Lots of people say that, but that doesn't mean someone feels comfortable bringing personal stuff into another person's office. I told my team: "You can come in to talk to me anytime. However, before coming in my door, let me know in advance that you're coming. Tell me what you're coming in for so I can be in the right frame of mind to help you best." I suggested the following as reasons for coming to see me:

- I need to vent (Your venting goes in a round box, and I don't remember it after you leave my office.)
- I have a problem and need coaching to find solutions.
- I need resources from you to solve a problem.

On a deeper level with more commitment to organizational equity, you might begin a Constructivist Listening program as described by Nanci Jimenez at LJList.com, to work through issues in work environments, social relationships, education programs, etc. Constructivist Listening is a timed listening activity where the speaker and listener have the same amount of time in each role: Speaker and listener. Constructivist Listening gives space for healing, deepens trust, and encourages the speaker to examine their own perceptions, make meaning for themselves, and trust their own mind to learn from their thoughts and experiences.

"We utilize Constructivist Listening as a core practice in our programs to engage in personal healing, increase confidence in our own abilities, and begin to make radical, revolutionary changes in how we relate to the people around us."

Nanci Jimenez, Luna Jimenez Institute
for Social Transformation

BEHAVIOR CHANGE HAPPENS WHEN WE REFLECT AND CREATE SHARED MEANING

DENISEism:
Eight Words to Success and Living Your Dream.

I was asked to speak to a group of 6th–12th graders attending a one-week college preparation course offered by the Charlotte Housing Authority, called Raising the Bar. I have to say that I speak to a lot of powerful executives and influential leaders, but there's no more difficult crowd than fifty preteens and teenagers gathered at 4:30 p.m. on a day where the temperature is hovering around 98 degrees!

As a speaker, you don't always know when you've done a good job. If you're a parent of young people in this age group, you know just how hard it is to know whether they're actually listening. Parenting, teaching, and coaching are acts of faith. Every time you speak to someone, you are taking a leap of faith that what you have to offer is just what they need. It's like the song: "He may not come when you want, but God is always on time."

I started my speech by saying, "You may not remember anything I have to say, but I hope these eight words will inspire you at the right moment to live your dreams. You see too many adults get to be old and then realize that they have bucket lists and then spend the rest of their lives trying to complete the list." As I ended with the last of the eight words, I thought the most exciting thing about my speech were the prizes I gave away during the speech. Imagine my surprise when Devon Campbell, 6th grade, approached me afterwards and handed me a paper showing how he used the eight words in a story about his dream.

DEVON'S DREAM

These eight words to success are really true. The eight words represent what we do now in school and out of school. Like "ideas." I get a lot of ideas and when I get them, I start planning. I "work" to fulfill my dream, which is to become the world's greatest game creator. All my life I have been caught up in games and some people say I'm addicted to it. And even people in school gave me the nickname "game freak." I am not very close to completing my goal yet, because I have to go to college to get my degree.

That's why I have "passion" for what I'm doing, and I made a "choice" to do this. I'll "push" myself every day. Every day to be the best. Dreaming about it every day. But I also know there is "value" in doing this. Also, I will "serve" others, like my teachers and guardians, so I can get help. I believe what you said about helping others (it will always come back to you). I will "persist" to get help so that I won't fall behind in completing my goal. Also, I do this to make my future the way I want it to be.

Speechless, I looked at Devon and thanked him. I got his permission to share his writing.

Denise's 8 Words for Success
Ideas
Work
Passion
Choice
Push
Value
Serve
Persist

As a speaker you always strive to be your best because it is a gift to be before others. Your job is to educate, entertain, and inspire. When the crowd is this young, constantly moving, talking, and fidgeting, it's easy to think no one is listening. Speaking before a crowd of fifty kids takes courage. Thanks, Devon, for reminding me that what we say matters, and someone is always listening.

REMARKABLE LEADERSHIP LESSONS

Sometimes people have to let the words sink in. We shouldn't judge our success by the immediate reaction of the person we're talking to.

- **Pause Strategically:** At the end of every meeting or interaction, if the person is giving you indications that they either weren't with you, didn't care, or blew you off, PAUSE, and then ask them what they're thinking.

We put our own spin on everything we see and hear based on our previous experience—which takes us to the Ladder of Conclusion.

- **The Ladder of Conclusion:** states that the way we view the world is through our historical experiences, and that we make inferences on what the other person is thinking based on our own experiences, and not the experience of the person with whom we are speaking.

Most people think all women like chocolate. I don't. But every year at Christmas, vendors would send me boxes and boxes of chocolate. I would use it to reward my staff, but I don't really know—maybe some of them didn't like chocolate either.

- **Plan for Expectation Hangovers:** Pam Brown, in her book *E-3*, talks about expectation hangovers. You go into something with great intentionality and then when it happens, it isn't what you expected. Sometimes it's better, sometimes worse, but what you're feeling is that you didn't accomplish what you thought for sure was going to happen.
- **Check for Understanding:** In all situations in your life, a universal best practice is to check for understanding, otherwise trust or distrust gets in the way. You know that meal you eat all the time that you hate because one time you were polite and then it's served every time you come to dinner? Don't have that happen in all areas of your life....
  - Check for shared meaning
  - Check for shared expectations

LIKE A STONE DROPPING INTO A POOL OF WATER, YOUR DECISIONS RIPPLE OR TIDALWAVE THROUGHOUT THE ORGANIZATION

I am finishing this book in the middle of the worst of times. The entire world has stopped because of COVID-19. For weeks now I have witnessed how online conversations have either; caused people to panic, or to create new opportunities for themselves and their families.

All of the change is generated by a conversation. I've noticed the ripple effects of those conversations and how they are changing us all in big and small ways. Like a drop of water makes a ripple in a pond, so do our conversations. We are always inspiring others. Each of us is a leader, an influencer in our own way. There is no denying that.

What it all comes down to is: What's the conversation in your head? What's the conversation you have with others? Are we kind with each other? Do we give the benefit of the doubt? Can we forgive ourselves for not being perfect, and then in turn, extend that act of forgiveness to others?

Thank you for reading all or some portion of my book. My hope is that wherever and whatever you read will inspire you to realize you have the capacity to change the world in both big and small ways. We are all connected, intertwined in ways seen and unseen.

I think the best thing that may come from this terrible time, is that many more people will realize the power they have to make a difference in someone's life. The power of your smile, word, frown, touch, and tone, can inspire someone to give more, engage more to make a difference, or to shut down and cut off. However you leave them, they too will affect someone else and so on and so on.

Know that you have an effect on everyone. Take steps toward becoming an impactful leader:

First step: Choose to be a positive influence and have the courage to challenge your own perceptions of what's right and wrong. Nothing happens without action.

Second step: Have the determination to step up, show up, and speak up.

Lastly: Know that success, peace, and happiness is a faith walk.

Like the ripples in a pond, you may not see when, where, or how they hit the shore. Coaching, mentoring, and developing others works the same way. There was a time that I didn't think I had that big an influence on others; I just did what I loved. Some people appreciated it and others didn't. Then, I spoke my stories and people like you asked me to write them down and share them. Your presence, your support and belief in me keeps me faithfully offering encouragement, resources, and sometimes a word of advice in the hopes that you will do the same for someone else. If we all do that, who knows what the next conversation will bring? Who knows how listening to another person's perspective can change the world?

Let us all understand that each of us has the power to change results, one conversation at a time.

ADDENDUM A:
TAKING HR TO THE NEXT LEVEL

Understanding the talent needs within your organization is more than measuring the impact of hiring, and taking the time to identify, assess, and understand the implications of the overall strategy on your people, and how skilled executives and managers are implementing the strategy. Talent management is an activity that can (and should) be measured, otherwise, your executives will not take it seriously.

Peter Drucker is often quoted as saying that, "You can't manage what you can't measure." What he meant is that, you can't know whether or not you are successful unless success is defined and tracked.

The focus of a strategic HR department, should be to help managers at all levels make decisions and act in ways that balance the needs of employees at every level, and every function. It starts with identifying people and organizational/functional capabilities needed, and the implications of not having them.

Human resource professionals, as well as every people manager at every level, should be able to answer the following strategic questions:

- What are the core skills, knowledge, and abilities our department/organization has to have to effectively meet the business tactics?
- What and where do we need specific talent, abilities, and/or flexibility to be prepared for future scenarios and business plans?
- If we aren't sufficiently capable, then what are the implications?
- If we did it right, what would be different? What results would we see on a regular basis?

The next step is assessing current talent within the organization. Human Resource professionals along with senior executives should be able to speak openly and transparently when they describe the following:

- Describe the current skill base (individual capabilities and collective capabilities).
- For each key strategic objective, what tactics must be accomplished to achieve results, and how will we know we have achieved them?
- What anticipated external social, demographic, and technological trends would fuel our ability to achieve our business tactics?
- What anticipated external social, demographic, and technological trends would prevent us from achieving our business tactics?
- Across the organization, what resources are available to achieve our business results?
- What have we learned over the past twelve months, and how did we do in anticipating, capitalizing, and mitigating the impact of change?

The next step would be talk about the gaps between where you want to go and where you are now. Afterwards, ask yourself: What do we want to tackle?

THE MEANING OF WORK

For decades, HR and executives have added all kinds of benefits, rewards, performance schemes, and a whole host of other techniques designed to improve productivity and employee engagement.

We have forgotten the meaning of work. Work gives us the ability to be self-sufficient first and foremost. Second it gives us the opportunity to do something meaningful. When executives forget or design corporate cultures that minimize the need for people to able to live well, and contribute to something bigger, more meaningful than themselves, that's when we all lose.

Engagement scores have been the same since their inception. Engagement scores are an indication of how much effort people are making to work smart, to dedicate their attention, brainpower, and creativity, towards helping a business engineer a better way of doing things.

At any point about 12–15 percent of employees are highly engaged, and about 80 percent are disengaged. Nearly 15 percent of the disengaged are actively disrupting the workplace. The reason CEOs are skeptical of their human resource efforts is because we've been measuring this number since the mid-1990s, and it hasn't changed. Most HR professionals keep justifying their expenditures as a way to keep businesses out of court, and/or preventing lawsuits.

HR, I hope, will evolve away from just transactional functions, and hiring and outplacement, and become part of the strategy of an organization. If HR is given the mandate to work towards breaking down barriers with the goal of aiding communication, and coworker relationships to thrive in the workplace, then much of the content of my coaching conversations throughout the anecdotes herein, can be incorporated into HR mentoring and coaching within organizations.

HR should be able to add value by directly impacting the employee engagement scores and retention. With a change in skill set and vision, HR would be able to train, mentor, and cultivate leaders from within their organizations. HR should continue to be involved in ongoing evaluations, skill assessments, and relationship cultivation within the organization. Or, if the HR team is limited in size or background, they could manage a network of coaches to be brought in as an accepted public, confidential enhancement of education, and training for current and emerging leaders.

CASE HISTORIES THAT CAN HELP YOU ASSESS AND UNDERSTAND HOW YOUR PEOPLE PROCESSES ARE REALLY WORKING

How capable are your employees when it comes to managing their boss's opinion about their performance?

- Velinda (p. 85)
- Lucas (p. 96),

Does your training help employees learn how to expand their ability to work with people unlike themselves?

- Sarah (p. 46)
- Sandra (p. 117)

What are the stories and messages people share when asked what it takes to do well at every level, and how well is your management team handling the politics of succession?

- Imani (p. 13)
- Surviving the shark frenzy (p. 141)

What are the stories people tell or reasons they give that let you know how others will behave when faced with difficult decisions? Will they do the right thing when no one is looking? Will they be kind, concerned, and supportive when called upon?

- Broken Heart Syndrome (p. 158)
- Catch Me If You Can (p. 150)

How is performance defined, measured, and managed?

- Arlen (p. 104)
- Lucas (p. 96)

Which stories address the value of people being able to ask all kinds of questions (even the dumb, potentially offensive ones?)

- Sophomore Year in College (p. xxxii)
- Kids Say the Darnedest Things (p. xxxvi)

ADDENDUM B: EXERCISES AND OTHER MATERIAL

ACTIVE LISTENING

A major part of my business is helping leaders connect to their feelings and senses, then helping them understand what their gut is actually trying to tell them. Our instinctual reaction is the first clue, but too often we rely on an unexamined story in our decision-making.

Being human means using all of our senses and brainpower. Being remarkable comes when you use all your senses and brainpower to be right more often than not. You become the go-to person. When others need help, your reputation defines what you have done that solves the problem. People like their problems to go away. Be that person who gets things done.

The next time you meet with a coworker, colleague, or your boss, try listening to what they are actually saying without adding your interpretation of what is meant. This is the first step in active listening.

ACTIVE LISTENING: CREATING A SHARED MEANING

The next time you're called into a meeting or have a regular update with your boss, practice active listening and paying attention to your senses.

The setup: At the beginning of the meeting ask for permission to do something a bit different.

I often tell my clients, tell your boss or colleague you want to do something different because you are working on developing new skills—in this case, active listening. **Get focused to Gain Insight.** Ask:

- What would make this a great meeting for you? Whatever the person says, ask:
- Why is that important? Whatever the person says, ask:
- What's the opportunity if we achieve that? Whatever the person says, ask:
- How does that serve the organization (or the department or the client)?

RELATIONSHIPS MATTER

In this case, the relationship I want you to focus on is with yourself. Notice how you felt asking the questions.

- How did your body respond or signal you at the beginning, middle, and end of the questioning?
- What did you notice about the other person—their body language and their tone of voice?
- What did you sense from them—comfort, joy, nervousness, relaxation, impatience, hope, annoyance, confusion, discomfort, possibly frustration towards the end?
- After the meeting, write out how you felt and what you learned. Was it a better meeting for you, for the other person, or for both of you?

EXERCISE: ARE YOU A VISIONARY LEADER OR A STRATEGIC IMPLEMENTER?

Walt Disney needed his brother Roy to make the Disney we know today all happen. Every visionary leader needs an implementer to see the details and help them make sure progress is being made.

Questions:

- Ask ten people to give you words or phrases that describe you at your best and at your worst. What patterns emerge?
- What are the skills, behaviors, and value others see in you?
- What do you find hard to believe, shy away from, or dismiss?
- What do you see as easy to believe and embrace about yourself?

ADDENDUM C: DENISEISMS

ACKNOWLEDGEMENTS

*"The moment you doubt whether you can fly,
you cease for ever to be able to do it."*

Peter Pan, J. M. Barrie

This quote from Peter Pan, the boy who never aged and could fly, means so much to me. I've been able to fly and glean the wisdom age brings because so many people shared a part of themselves with me. Some I've known for a short time, some forever, and I've grown to know that it is not the length of time but the generosity that lives in a person's heart that matters.

I want to first thank my family, who kept faith in me and whose wisdom ground me every day, making it possible to have great conversations with others. The list is long, and each person is special to me.

My dad, Albert L. Williams, who taught me to aspire to do anything and balance the desire to "do" with the reality of "achieving" without breaking my spirit. Ms. Louise, my mom, who taught me you can say anything; it's all in how you say it. My grandparents taught me the value of working hard and to never stop trying no matter what you see in front of you. My Aunt Karen Howard told me I was beautiful even when I didn't believe it, and her husband Phil Howard, instilled in me a sense of pride in those who came before us and that each of us stands on a puzzle piece. I learned from Uncle Phil that if we play our part well, all of us are lifted up closer to God's dream.

To my brother Anthony and sister Anita who taught me more about perspective than anyone else, thank you for being in my life.

To my children, Regina and Shanita. Thank you for teaching me to be careful what I wish for because God has a wicked sense of humor.

To my amazing, rock steady, always got my back girlfriends, Connie Bailey, Donah Ollila, Susan Couslin, and Deanna Watts. Each of you taught me what love and forgiveness look like and how to embrace self-care without shame or apology.

For all the moments I've spent with some of the most incredible souls in the world, I am grateful. This book is a small attempt to repay the countless people who have contributed to my personal and professional growth, as well as for the stories and content they've contributed to this book.

Words cannot express my deepest and heartfelt gratitude to my clients, friends, and my invisible board of advisors, supporters, and mentors. My life lessons are the gifts you shared with me, and this book is my humble attempt to honor your words, spirit, struggle, and hope that together we can achieve something extraordinary. You shared your stories, some in confidence, and yet in my eyes, you are the most remarkable leaders around. Quietly developing yourself and extending your love, wisdom, and guidance to those appreciative, and (like me) sometimes blind recipients of the gifts you offered.

This book would not even be here if it weren't for all the people who came up to me after a speech and said, "Do you have a book? You need a book! I want to learn more from you." It wouldn't be possible if people like Glenn Proctor, Carla Carlisle, Paula Lesso, and Pamela Lue-Hing for taking their time to coach, encourage, and nudge me to keep at it.

If there is any wisdom in this book, people like Pamela Brooks-Richardson, Deborah Snow-Walsh, Brian and Lou Raye Nichol, and Harvey Smith taught me so much about coaching, recruiting, and myself.

Thank you, Fern Pessin, for helping me find my voice and knowing that I have so many stories to share, but more importantly, I should appreciate my own stories. They really are the building blocks of greatness.

Thank you to the dedicated and talented staff at Publish Your Purpose Press. Jenn Grace, Heather B. Habelka, and Bailly Morse. Their suggestions, support, and especially all of their excitement about my stories, kept me believing this book was worth publishing. The gift you give is granting voice to ordinary people with extraordinary stories to tell.

I want to acknowledge and say a "big thank you" to my weekly spiritual reflections group. Elizabeth Gibbons, William Spencer, and Cyndi Krupp. We have been together for over 8 years, having conversations about how to live fully in our faith's beliefs. We continue our faith walk knowing that we are connected and becoming all the time.

To my South Dakota crew, Rev. Marchelle Hallman, Pastor Rev. Angelo V. Chatmon, Desmond Rogers, Elaine Miles, Michelle Hearon, Sheila Brown, and Gail "Lady B" Baker. The days we spent then and our reunion taught me so much about the power of perspective, the voices in our heads, and that Godwinks are everywhere and in everything no matter what we see in front of us.

Finally, I thank God for the lessons and blessings Ivan G. Hall has brought before me. Your words have taught me that I don't have to know it for sure. That not having experienced certain things in life has shaped me as much as the things I have gone through. You can have lots of reasons/excuses or results, but you can't have both.

Forgive me if I didn't acknowledge you by name. Know that you are in my heart, and I respect your request for privacy and appreciate so much the brilliant advice you shared with me.

I hope that those who read the words in this book will stop long enough to look around and realize no one is alone. No one achieves anything without others in their corner, and that just because they don't broadcast their support doesn't mean they aren't cheering, guiding, and helping to mold you into a wise, kind, giving, and brilliant person.